THE
ANOINTING AND YOU
UNDERSTANDING REVIVAL

David Walters

Published by
GOOD NEWS FELLOWSHIP MINISTRIES
220 Sleepy Creek Road
Macon GA 31210
Phone:(478)757-8071
Fax:(478)757-0136
e-mail:goodnews@reynoldscable.net
www.goodnews.netministries.org

Good News Fellowship Ministries
220 Sleepy Creek Road
Macon GA 31210

Unless otherwise quoted, all Scripture quotations are
from the New King James Version of the Bible
Copyright © 1979,1980,1982
by Thomas Nelson Inc., publishers
Used by permission.

Printed by :
Faith Printing
4210 Locust Hill Road
Taylors S.C. 29687

Contents

Introduction

In January of 1996, I was asked to do a series of teachings on the Holy Spirit with a church in Alaska. The main focus of my ministry is usually to parents, children and youth, and children/youth pastors. The pastor asked if I would teach the whole church on this subject. Although this and other churches in Alaska where I had preached had visits from Rodney Howard-Browne and his brother, Bazil, they were hungry to learn more of the anointing. We had five days of teaching, and it turned out to be a blessed time for all.

Because of the success of those meetings and the receptivity from those who attended, I felt the Holy Spirit impress me to write a book on the subjects that I covered. Although this book is called *The Anointing and You*, it is somewhat different from other books written on the same subject. Listed below are some of the topics covered.

1.   How to understand the anointing.

2. Why some people receive and some don't.

3. How to continue with a fresh anointing after we have initially received it.

4. How churches can bring the anointing to others.

5. How we impart the anointing to others.

6. How we can channel the anointing to go beyond the initial falling down and laughing, etc.

7. How to pass it on to the next generation.

I trust this book will answer many questions that you, the reader, may have regarding the anointing. Prayerfully meditate upon the revelation and keys in this book. I believe that it will help you, and your church, into His Anointing for renewal and revival.

I personally have seen many churches come into revival, when I have had the privilege of ministering. So often God has used the children. The wise churches adjusted their wineskins to accommodate that fresh anointing and are still experiencing renewal today. May you and your church join the happy ranks.

David Walters

CHAPTER ONE

Understanding the Anointing

The anointing is the hand of God upon His people. The touch of God is all that it takes to transform lives. The anointing turns wimps into warriors, chickens into champions, dorks into dragon slayers, and ordinary people become extraordinary.

Samson, the strongest man in the Bible, was **not** famous for his muscles. The secret of his great strength that enabled him to defeat his enemies was not that he had a physique like Arnold Schwarzenegger, but the anointing. Every time Samson performed a great feat it says the Spirit of the Lord came upon him. *"And the Spirit of the Lord came mightily upon him, and he tore the lion apart as one would have torn apart a young goat, though he had nothing in his hand..."* (**Judg. 14:6**).

Many Christians claim they are weak, many believe that they don't have enough faith to accomplish much. If we can believe in what we don't have, then why not believe in what we do have? It is better to have faith in the positive, rather than the negative. We must **never** believe that our weaknesses are stronger than God's power. This is what we do, when we claim that God can't really use us much, because of our spiritual frailty. *"But God has chosen the foolish things of the world to put to shame the wise, and God has chosen the weak things of the world to put to shame the things which are mighty"* **(1 Cor. 1:27).** When we understand, receive, and rely on the anointing, we can accomplish greater feats in the spiritual realm than Samson ever did in the natural.

I was saved in 1959, but it wasn't until ten years later that I was ready to be filled or baptized in the Holy Spirit. Like many believers, I had struggled with attempting to live a victorious Christian life. I felt that I was parked in Romans 7, *"For the good that I will to do, I do not do; but the evil I will not to do, that I practice"* **(Rom. 7:19).** I did not know how to go on into Romans 8. *"There is therefore now no condemnation to those who are in Christ Jesus, who do not walk according to the flesh, but according to the Spirit"* **(Rom. 8:1).** I believed that if I could have victory over the flesh, it would qualify me to walk in the Spirit. I did not realize that it is by **faith that I can** walk in the Spirit, which is my deliverance from a carnal walk. Failing, confessing, trying, and failing again was a wearisome pattern. A number of great saints seemed to have achieved that happy state of almost unbroken fellowship and victorious living, but it seemed to elude lesser mortals like myself. I was woeful of my condition, and found it hard to accept that after ten years as a Christian, I was still unable to achieve victory over the flesh. I had even read books on the *Crucified Life*. But I was unable to crucify myself. Every time I managed to nail one hand to the cross, I couldn't get it free to nail the other hand. I tried imagining that I was dead, but it didn't work. The idea of living the crucified life did not really appeal to me. Although water baptism is a burial, it is illegal to bury people that are not yet dead. What I had not yet seen was that the "Resurrected Life" should have been my final goal. Death comes before burial and burial comes before resurrection. It is **not** dying to self and living for Christ, but dying to self and allowing Christ to live in me and through me. *"To them God willed to make known what are the riches of the glory of this mystery among the Gentiles: which is Christ in you, the hope of glory"* **(Col. 1:27).**

I knew that I lacked power, I did not feel that I was Spirit-filled, and I was constantly looking within myself to find something good and acceptable to God. Every time I felt that I had failed, I prayed the same prayer over and over again. *"Create in me a clean heart, O God, And renew a steadfast spirit within me"* **(Psalm 51:10).** Just prior to coming into the Spirit-filled life, the Lord began to orchestrate things. Kathie and I began praying with another couple for the infilling of the Holy Spirit. Previously our pastor, Dr. D.M. Lloyd-Jones, had preached on the Baptism of the Holy Spirit for six months. Unfortunately, his Calvinism came out in his messages, as he instructed us to seek the baptism, but said we may not receive it because God is sovereign and He may or may not oblige us. It was only much later that I realized, when Jesus said, *"Ask, and it will be given to you; seek, and you will find; knock, and it will be opened to you"* **(Matt. 7:7).** He did not say **might** in front of ask! seek! and knock! but **shall.**

Dr. Martyn Lloyd-Jones had now retired, but we were still praying and seeking. One of the sisters we were praying with had come across a book in a secondhand bookstore called *The Normal Christian Life* by Watchman Nee. Although we had never heard of him before, we began to devour the book. Then there was another book that came across our path. A book about prayer by Andrew Murray began to affect us. One must realize that almost all of the religious books we had previously read regarding doctrine were from the reformed camp.

The newest thing that occurred was that Ralph, the person who had led me to the Lord, suddenly appeared on our doorstep one Saturday morning. As we invited him in, he began to witness to Kathie and I about being baptized in the Holy Spirit. Just before he left he asked me if I was filled with the Spirit. I said, "No." He then said, "Do you believe that God can fill you with the Spirit?" "Yes," I replied. "Do you believe that God **will** fill you with the Spirit?" "That, I'm not sure of!" I said. "You **must** believe that He will," replied Ralph. "How will I know if He will?" I asked. "When you believe, you will know." Those last words that Ralph said before he left rang through my ears.

I went upstairs to the bedroom and began to pray my usual prayer. "Create in me a clean heart, etc." Then the Lord reminded me of the children of Israel, trapped by the Red Sea with Pharaoh's armies ready to descend on them. He then said to me, "Stand still and see My salvation. Stop trying and start trusting." I began to see that there was nothing in me that was of any value to God. He did not want to **change** me, He wanted to **exchange** me. I was too far gone to be salvaged. I needed to be willing to die, give up and surrender and accept the fact that there was nothing in me that was pleasing to God. When I accepted that fact, I began to rejoice. No longer was I trying to present to God something worthy or virtuous in me. It was no longer I, but Christ. *"I have been crucified with Christ; it is no longer I who live, but Christ lives in me; and the life which I now live in the flesh I live by faith in the Son of God, who loved me and gave Himself for me"* **(Gal. 2:20).**

God had dealt with my subconscious pride that could not accept the fact that there was nothing in my religious life that was acceptable to God. Now instead of bemoaning my sins, I was rejoicing. For years my evangelical friends and I would tell God and each other what miserable sinners and how unworthy we were. We thought we were being spiritual. But now I saw that for years I had been sin conscious, rather than Christ conscious. Within a few short weeks many of our friends came into the same experience, as they also saw that they were dead to sin and alive to Christ. Even though we had seen that in the Scriptures, it had never come alive before.

*"For the law of the Spirit of life in Christ Jesus **has made me free from the law of sin and death"*** **(Rom. 8:2).** I like that word **has**, not will, but **has.** The law of sin and death is like the law of gravity. It keeps us earthbound. We can never be free from the law of gravity, in the same way we can never be free from the law of sin and death. Many times Christians had said, "If only I was not disposed to do wrong, it would be wonderful," but the power of temptation is always there. Because we can never be free from the law of gravity, there is another law that comes

11

into operation which supersedes the law of gravity. It is the law of aerodynamics which keeps a plane flying. So in the same way, the law of the Spirit of life in Christ Jesus keeps us free from the law of sin and death.

As I was asking the Lord to fill me, I felt a hand gently pushing me down from my kneeling position at the side of my bed, till I was flat on the floor. Even then, although I wanted God's presence and power, I was frightened of this feeling of losing control. For God to absolutely rule in our lives is something most Christians don't experience.

When I preach to children, I often do a little scenario. I call a boy up to the platform and sit him in a chair. The chair represents a throne and he is the king. He hears about Jesus. He then sees that if he wants to go to heaven he must ask Christ into his heart. He decides to invite Christ in. He moves across on the chair and makes room for the Lord. I sit down and share his chair with him. Remember the chair represents the throne. I represent Christ. He now has Christ, but he is still partly running his own life, and up to a point, he can still do his thing. As I sit there, I say to him, "Son, this is not quite what I planned, I did not come to share the throne with you, I came to take over." I then shove him off the chair and he falls to the floor. I then say to the congregation, "Little Jimmy is no longer in charge, Jesus is. What then happens to Jimmy?" I pick him up, stand behind him and stretch his hands out. "Jesus was on the cross and Jimmy was on the throne. Now Jesus is on the throne of Jimmy's heart and Jimmy goes on the cross. Bye! Bye! Jimmy, welcome Jesus!" It is not an **amalgamation** that Jesus Christ seeks with us, but our **abdication.**

It would be great to say that since then I have had complete victory and unbroken fellowship with the Lord. I have learned that nothing is automatic, and unless I stay in faith and obedience I will fall back to walking in the flesh. On the occasions when I have disappointed myself by messing up, just when I thought I was doing so well, the Lord has reminded me that in my flesh nature I will never improve. God did not come to perfect the old man, but to show me how to walk in the new man. *"For I know that in me (that is, in my flesh) nothing good dwells; for to will is present with me, but how to perform what is good I do not find"* **(Rom. 7:18).** All sin comes from **unbelief.** If I believe that my fleshy emotions and appetites are more powerful than the Holy Spirit then I succumb, but when I trust that God's power and anointing will see me through, then I have the victory. Everything we do comes by faith. Let us look not only to a **saving** God, but also to a **keeping** God. *"Now to Him who is able to **keep** you from stumbling, And to present you faultless Before the presence of His glory with exceeding joy"* **(Jude 24).**

When God created man and woman, His original purpose was for them to bear fruit. *"Then God blessed them, and God said to them, 'Be fruitful and multiply; fill the earth and subdue it; have dominion over the fish of the sea, over the birds of the air, and over every living thing that moves on the earth"* **(Gen. 1:28).** The birthing of children was to bring forth a race of people that would reflect God's glory. Remember we are made in His image and likeness. **(See Gen. 1:26.)** As we know, Satan tried to ruin God's purpose by bringing about the downfall of man.

The Holy Spirit who is the "Anointed One" brought forth the church on the day of Pentecost and commissioned her to be fruitful, multiply and fill the Kingdom. A kingdom must not only have a king, but subjects to reign over. When Mary was visited by the angel Gabriel, she was told that she was to become the mother of Jesus. How was this to be? *"...The Holy Spirit will come upon you, and the power of the Highest will overshadow you; therefore, also, that Holy One who is to be born will be called the Son of God"* **(Luke 1:35).**

As the Holy Spirit entered into Mary's womb and she became spiritually pregnant, so when we receive Christ, we also become spiritually pregnant. This new life that we now possess is expected to grow, develop and be brought forth. *"My little children, for whom I labor in birth again until Christ is formed in you"* **(Gal. 4:19).** Paul is seeing himself as a midwife taking part in the birthing; a birthing for Christ to be formed in us. Unfortunately for many Christians, Christ seems to be deformed in them, rather than formed.

In the spiritual realm, the reproductive organ is the mouth. The seed is the Word of God. **(See Matt. 13:19-23.)** When we preach under the anointing, the seed comes out of our mouths and goes into the ears of the hearers. If the seed (Word) takes root in their hearts, then they become pregnant with the Holy Spirit and a new child is on the way. As there is no age in the spiritual realm, young and old alike can bring forth children. I often tell little boys and girls that they can become spiritual moms and dads. If they tell their friends about Christ, and their friends accept Him, then they have brought forth children. It is wonderful that we all, old

14

and young alike, are called to be fruitful and multiply and fill the Kingdom.

As Adam and Eve were made in the image of God, the Holy Spirit is the one that conforms us to the image of Christ. *"For whom He foreknew, He also predestined to be conformed to the image of His Son, that He might be the firstborn among many brethren"* **(Rom. 8:29).** Although the Bible is of utmost importance, it is not knowing Bible verses alone that will change us. Some people make the mistake by saying the Bible is the Word of God. This is not strictly true. It is God's record and it contains His Word, but it also contains the words of man and the words of Satan. Jesus was not talking about the Bible, He was talking about God's word in the Bible, when He said to Satan, *"...It is written, 'Man shall not live by bread alone, but by every word that proceeds from the mouth of God' "* **(Matt. 4:4).** It is the very word of God that declares that the Spirit of God transforms us into the image of Christ. *"But we all, with unveiled face, beholding as in a mirror the glory of the Lord, are being transformed into the same image from glory to glory, just as by the Spirit of the Lord"* **(2 Cor. 3:18).**

It is so important that we first understand the Holy Spirit Anointing. God does **not** anoint the flesh. For example, true unity can only come from the anointing. *"Behold, how good and how pleasant it is For brethren to dwell together in unity! It is like the precious oil upon the head, Running down on the beard, The beard of Aaron, Running down on the edge of his garments"* **(Psalm 133:1-2).** Notice the oil never touched Aaron's flesh, but only his hair and garments. The Holy Spirit only brings forth God's plan, not man's. He will not support our agenda, no matter how good it seems or how sincere and dedicated we are.

There have been many times when preaching in church meetings, that I have to ask the Holy Spirit to forgive us. Because it seems so many times we have insulted the Holy Spirit by **not** asking Him to take control of our meetings. After repenting, I then ask Him to honor us with His presence. There is nothing like it. When He comes, it is so glorious, and He does desire to come, as long as we make ourselves and our meetings available to Him. Let's not allow our churches to be like the story of the preacher who was complaining to God because a certain church would not let him come and minister. Apparently the Holy Spirit said, "I know how you feel, I have been trying to get into that church for years." We have sung the song many times, "Holy Spirit, You are welcome in this place." Not only must we welcome Him in our churches, but also in our lives. We can so easily insult Him when we don't allow Him to have free access to our beings. Some may argue that if the Holy Spirit is everywhere, then he must be present in our church. True, but most times He is not manifested everywhere. We allow Him to watch, but not to participate.

The Holy Spirit's Anointing is the opposite to dryness, deadness, self-consciousness, struggle, burn-out, fear, failure, poverty, and sickness. Why put up with so many of these negatives, when He wants to pour out His anointing upon us? What I unfold in the following chapters will require faith to work in our daily lives. Simple childlike faith is the key to all that God has for us. Whether we talk in tongues, witness, move in the other spiritual gifts, pray, or worship, we need to activate our faith. We often say that love is the greatest, agreed; but faith is the first. **(See 1 Cor. 13:13.)** Faith is the springboard for everything else to function. If we do anything without faith, no matter how noble, it will be of no use. We could also be sinning. *"But he who doubts is condemned if he eats, because he does not eat from faith; for whatever is not from faith is sin"* **(Rom. 14:23).** *"But without faith it is impossible to please Him, for he who comes to God must believe that He is, and that He is a rewarder of those who diligently seek Him"* **(Heb. 11:6).**

Let us break forth from the hindrances of the flesh and mind realm and reach out in the Spirit. Let us be like the eagles, that launch out on the wind currents to fly to greater heights. We are not called to be earthbound chickens. There may be many church people who will try to tie us down to the mundane and the boring in the interest of safety. To really rely on the Holy Spirit can be scary at first, but it will be exciting. You may even think you are the only one, but as you begin to fly, you will find others alongside you. You may only be a remnant, or a Gideon company, but you will succeed.

CHAPTER TWO

Receiving the Anointing

God is pouring out His Spirit in many parts of the world today. Numbers of us who live in the U.S. and the western world are also receiving refreshing and revival, and it is increasing in a number of places, yet many are still not experiencing His outpouring. Among those of us who are claiming God's blessing, some in our ranks are only receiving a pale shadow of what He really desires for His church. When I have ministered to people, from children and teens to adults, I have often been disappointed. Many have claimed they are "Spirit filled" yet their faces and words don't show it. When I see this, I ask the question, "Is this that which was spoken by the prophet Joel?" It doesn't appear so to me. *"But this is what was spoken by the prophet Joel: 'And it shall come to pass in the last days, says God, That I will pour out of My Spirit on all flesh; Your sons and your daughters shall prophesy, Your young men shall see visions, Your old men shall dream dreams'"* **(Acts 2:16-17).**

We are living in the last days and the promise is that God's outpouring is for young and old alike. Notice the Scripture says, *"I will pour out of My Spirit on all flesh."* Not adult flesh only, or Bible scholars only, but **all** flesh. Although many of us may experience something of God's outpouring and be overcome momentarily by the presence of His Holy Spirit, it's only when we repent and open ourselves up for Him to enter in and control our lives, that we will be permanently changed.

I remember many years ago when a student came into a meeting which we were having. The presence of the Lord was very strong. As this young man (who was not a Christian) entered into the room, he was knocked down and was overcome by the Lord's presence in a remarkable way. After the meeting was over, he was completely beside himself. "I have never experienced anything like that in my life! It was awesome!" he said. "Praise God," we thought, "another one added to the Lord," but we were wrong! Even though we encouraged him to come back and be discipled, he wasn't interested. We finally realized that the Spirit had come upon him, but had **not** taken residence in him. He had not repented. The result of repentance and water baptism is to be filled with the Holy Spirit. *"...And you shall receive the gift of the Holy Spirit. For the promise is to you and to your children, and to all who are afar off, as many as the Lord our God will call"* **(Acts 2:38-39).**

We have had the privilege of seeing God pour out His Spirit on children as young as three or four years of age, on church wise and rebellious teenagers, on adults and the elderly. If people stay in the presence of the Holy Spirit long enough, sooner or later He will arrest them. For some it may take a few minutes, hours, or days; others, many weeks or months. The Holy Spirit's convicting power is not to condemn, but to bring about repentance and deliverance. The Holy Spirit takes the word "preached" and gives it power. If the preaching is God's truth, then the Holy Spirit will bear witness to it, because He is the Spirit of Truth. **(See John 14:17.)** God will confirm **His** word with accompanying signs, not our words. **(See Mark 16:20.)**

Notice the Holy Spirit will not bear witness to clever sermons or moving messages unless they are coming from the heart of God. The Holy Spirit does **not** bear witness to that which is **true,** but that which is the **truth**. We can preach orthodox sermons that are true and doctrinally correct, but it may not be what God is saying at the time. Many old-style churches traditionally preach a gospel service on Sunday night, even though the congregation has been saved for 20 years! For some preachers it doesn't make any difference what the Holy Spirit wants to do, they are determined to keep the tradition. *"Who also made us sufficient as ministers of the new covenant, not of the letter but of the Spirit; for the letter kills, but the Spirit gives life"* **(2 Cor. 3:6).** The Holy Spirit can do more in a few seconds than we can accomplish in years. Often people have come for counseling and after many months, or even years, little progress seems to be made, yet one touch from the Holy Spirit can change their lives and put them on the right course.

I was speaking at a church in Ohio one time. One of the visitors at the meetings was a leader in the "Way" movement, which is a cult. His wife had become a Christian and he had come to check it out. He was also a medical doctor, a heart specialist. The power of the Holy Spirit so arrested him during that meeting that he received the Lord and was delivered from his cult practices. He said that he had never experienced God in such a tangible way. A year or so later when I returned to that church, he was a very active member, still rejoicing in his salvation. It was the power and presence of the Holy Spirit that made the difference. He saw and experienced something more than doctrinal arguments.

We Must Be Hungry

To receive the power of the Holy Spirit or God's anointing in our lives and the life of the church we must be hungry and thirsty. The book of Matthew says, *"Blessed are those who hunger and thirst for righteousness, For they shall be filled"* (**Matt. 5:6**). There is a principle here; anything that we desire from God requires hungering and thirsting. Then the promise is that we shall be filled. *"Ask, and it will be given to you; seek, and you will find; knock, and it will be opened to you"* (**Matt. 7:7**). Not maybe, but yes. *"For all the promises of God in Him are Yes, and in Him Amen . . ."* (**2 Cor. 1:20**). *"...Was not Yes and No, but in Him was Yes"* (**2 Cor. 1:19**).

Some people have become disillusioned when asking for the anointing or the gift of tongues or other gifts, because they have been unable to receive; they then conclude that these gifts are **not** for everyone. Their attitude is, "Well, we don't have to have this. It is not really necessary and because I have not been baptized in the Spirit or speak in other tongues, that doesn't make me inferior to those who do, so gifts and anointing are not such a big deal."

Why is it that some people receive and others don't? In most cases it's to do with the intensity of the desire and the knowledge of how to receive. So let's deal first with the desire. Only hungry and thirsty people eat and drink. If we are not really hungry or thirsty, we will be more concerned about what tickles our palate, rather than satisfying a craving. We will be picky. "I'm not sure what I really want to eat." "Nothing on the menu really appeals to me." "What kind of drinks do you have?" "Is it sugar free?" "Does it have caffeine?" "Go easy on the ice." "I need a straw, I can't drink soda without a straw." This would not be the reaction of starving people, or those that were dying of thirst.

I remember when my girls were small and we would be walking through a park on a hot summer day. "Daddy! Daddy! I'm dying of thirst, I need a drink," one of them would say. "I can't help you, there aren't any soda machines," was my reply. "But Daddy, I'm dying of thirst!" A few minutes later, after putting up with the complaints, I would see a water fountain. "Now you can have a drink," I would exclaim. "But Daddy, I want Coca Cola." "I thought you were thirsty?" "I am! I am! But I want Coca Cola." Like most children, she wasn't really dying of thirst.

When we become really desperate, we don't get picky. We won't start to dictate to God how and when we want our blessing and what form it should take. We will be like the Canaanite woman who reminded Jesus that even the dogs eat the crumbs that fall from the master's table. **(See Matt. 15:27.)** Some people have a measure of the Spirit, or a measure of blessing, so they see no need for more. God's desire is that we should have fullness, but if we are content with measure, then we will not desire fullness. *"And of His **fullness** we have all received, and grace for grace"* (**John 1:16**). *"To know the love of Christ which passes knowledge; that you may be filled with all the **fullness** of God"* (**Eph. 3:19**). *"Till we all come to the unity of the faith and the knowledge of the Son of God, to a perfect man, to the measure of the stature of the **fullness** of Christ"* (**Eph. 4:13**). *"For He whom God has sent speaks the words of God, for God does not give the Spirit by **measure**"* (**John 3:34**). The satisfaction with measure is not only true for individuals, but also for churches. The greatest enemy of fullness is measure, and good becomes the enemy of God. We become satisfied with something good and miss God. Those who have **nothing** usually know it, and that can be an advantage.

There are some church leaders who use the following arguments. "We have good services, attendance, sermons and good offerings; we don't need anything more." So good replaces the best and measure takes the place of fullness. If we aren't careful, we can become like the Laodicean church, which the Lord rebuked. *"I know your works, that you are neither cold nor hot. I could wish you were cold or hot. So then, because you are lukewarm, and neither cold nor hot, I will spew you out of My mouth. Because you say, 'I am rich, have become wealthy, and have need of nothing'— and do not know that you are wretched, miserable, poor, blind, and naked"* (**Rev. 3:15-17**).

There are many churches that like to be "balanced." What some mean by that is that they don't want to go into excess. "Do all things in moderation" is often their slogan. After all, Paul said, *"Let all things be done decently and in order"* (**1 Cor. 14:40**). Perhaps they **so** emphasize "decently and in order" that nothing much is **done** as far as the supernatural is concerned.

(This is obviously the opposite to the preacher who was accused of being excessive. "I probably am," he said. "My desire is to be excessively victorious, excessively holy, excessively pleasing to God, excessively healthy, excessively faithful and I want to see an excessive number of souls saved.")

"We don't want to go overboard, let's take the middle road." "We don't want to frighten people or put them off." "We must be sensitive to where they are at." "We want to reach this generation of yuppies, so let's have our 'seeker sensitive,' 'seeker friendly' services."

We are told by modern church growth experts, "The way to make your church grow is to apply the following: Make sure that your services do not last for more than one hour and 15 minutes. Make the altar call by not having an altar call, in other words do not embarrass people by asking them to come forward, but just let them receive Christ quietly in their hearts without others seeing. Do not have any spiritual gifts or supernatural happenings, as it could alarm the audience. Let them watch a good drama. Sit back, relax, and enjoy the show. Make sure you have good music and short, to the point, uplifting messages and a nice comfortable atmosphere. That will keep them coming back."

What do we say to this? Do we criticize these kind of churches? We must be careful not to judge the motives, because some are sincere and diligent in what they are doing. Many are getting excellent results in terms of people joining the church. Obviously drama, dance, professional presentations and modern techniques are not wrong, but we must be diligent in trusting the Holy Spirit and not restricting Him in our gatherings. If we are concerned that He might embarrass or upset our structured programs, then we will be the losers in the end.

There are two kinds of philosophy. One is that we should use every resource and talent that we have to produce excellence, and then pray for the Holy Spirit to bless it. The other is that all our efforts and talents are useless, unless the Holy Spirit has complete control. In fact, often He will do a better job than us, if we give up and let Him take over completely. There are dangers with both of these points of view if they are taken to **excess**. They could bring about the following problems:

1. The first position can cause us to develop a Messiah complex or works mentality. The emphasis is that it is up to us to save the world, perform, etc. The result of this striving will lead to frustration and burn-out, especially if we fail to achieve the desired results. On the other hand, if we are blessed with a measure of success, we probably will not feel inadequate, or see a need for revival. As previously said, a **measure** of blessing can keep us from desiring **fullness**. The greater talent and ability we leaders have, the less likely we are to see the need to completely rely on the Holy Spirit.

2. The other position can lead us to a kind of fatalism. We so emphasize the sovereignty of God that we fall into apathy and laziness. We profess that we can't do anything, for God has to do it all. Instead of seeing that God has ordained to work His power and plan through us, His people, we expect Him to do it for us, while we merely become spectators. We must remember that we are called to be coworkers with Him. *"We then, as workers together with Him also plead with you not to receive the grace of God in vain"* **(2 Cor. 6:1).** To conclude, we don't work alone, nor does God work alone, but He works through yielded dedicated vessels. *". . .Work out your own salvation with fear and trembling; for it is God who works in you both to will and to do for His good pleasure"* **(Phil. 2:12-13).**

The early church did not seem concerned about having "seeker sensitive" or "seeker friendly" services. The Apostle Peter did not seem to be too concerned about people being embarrassed! He rebuked two of the church members, Ananias and Sapphira, and they dropped down dead; the result of their dying was that, *". . . great fear came upon all the church and upon all who heard these things"* **(Acts 5:11).** The reactions to that awesome happening were that numbers of people, who at first appeared to be interested, were no longer willing to get involved. **(See Acts 5:13.)** (So much for being seeker friendly.) Yet, out of the supernatural manifestations, *". . . believers were increasingly added to the Lord, multitudes of both men and women"* **(Acts 5:14).** Many preachers have said that the Holy Spirit is a gentleman and He will never embarrass anyone. Not true! He embarrassed Ananias and Sapphira to death. **(See Acts 5:1-10.)**

When I preach to children and youth, many of them are like the Laodicean church. "Why are you bugging me? I am a Christian, I don't need or want anything more, leave me alone." "Can I go and play now?" They have a measure, but have no desire for fullness. They are lukewarm. Often it's because their friends are lukewarm, their parents are lukewarm, and their church is lukewarm. Even in cases where the churches and the parents are on fire, until they see other youngsters change, they will stay in that lukewarm condition. We have, by the grace of God, seen many of them turned around in our meetings, as the Word of God convicts them and the Holy Spirit falls on them. When some receive the anointing or renewal, others then open up to receive. When the children are stirred up, they become happy and excited and can't wait to attend every meeting. Our ministry is one of the most difficult; to reach gospel-hardened, church-wise kids and adults. Only the manifestation of the Holy Spirit can do it. That is why we must rely on the anointing.

Some people seem to receive the Holy Spirit easily and others seem to have a really hard time. Why is this? Could it be a question of attitude with some? We cannot go to a revival or renewal meeting with a critical attitude, trying to find out what is wrong with it; for if we do, Satan will accommodate us. We will soon find something going on that is not of the Lord. We must **not** throw the baby out with the bath water by saying, "This meeting is not of God, because I saw some unscriptural practices." Some may say, "I want a pure move, not a mixture." We must not reject every move of God and spend our whole lives waiting for the perfect situation. I don't believe that we will ever see a 100% pure move of God this side of heaven, because as soon as it hits

28

flesh, it becomes tainted. It's like saying, "I want to join a perfect church." If you could find one to join, you would spoil it. None of us are perfect. All the blessings and moves of God that are being showered upon us are in danger of being polluted, because of our fallen human nature.

Others may go to revival meetings with a cynical attitude. They don't believe it's real, just a bunch of foolishness. It is impossible for people to judge something that they have not experienced personally. There are some church-wise teenagers who sneer and mock at what God is doing, because they have no firsthand knowledge of what is happening. These cynical spectators often try to intimidate other youngsters who are interested in the move of God. A prophetic friend of mine recently said, "A man with an experience is never at the mercy of a man with an argument." That is why it is important for our Christian life to be real.

How to Receive

To experience God's anointing or blessing, to be revived or refreshed, we must be ready to receive. Many people and churches pray to God, asking Him to pour out His Spirit, but they don't know how to receive. God gives us His Holy Spirit, but we must **receive** Him. This is fundamental in every aspect of the Christian experience. *"For God so loved the world that He gave His only begotten Son . . ."* (**John 3:16**). *"But as many as **received** Him, to them He **gave** the right to become children of God . . ."* (**John 1:12**).

I remember many years ago when my wife, Kathie, and I were on vacation and we visited a little Pentecostal church. The pastor's wife had been tarrying for 30 years to receive the Baptism of the Spirit, but still hadn't received it. We offered to pray for her after giving her a little instruction on receiving **by faith**, and she was filled with the Holy Spirit. For 30 years religious demons had held her back from receiving God's blessing.

We must come in full assurance of faith. God is not impressed with our religious prayers. Crying out in desperation, with wailing, griping, handwringing, sobbing, beating our breasts, banging the floor, etc. God does not respond to this; it does not impress Him. He responds to our persevering faith, not our whining. *"Let us therefore come boldly to the throne of grace, that we may obtain mercy and find grace to help in time of need"* **(Heb. 4:16).** We who are parents, do not immediately respond to our children when they run to us for help and consolation after having some crisis. We first calm down their sobbing and screaming in order for them to be able to tell us what their need or their problem is. Once we understand their request, then we can help. I believe God responds in the same way to His children. He desires for us to be clear and specific. We are not trying to twist the arm of a reluctant God, as some people interpret knocking and seeking. We **are** expected to persevere in prayer, but that is more for our benefit than God's.

Kathie and I prayed for our parent's salvation for ten years. Finally God asked us when we were going to believe! When we prayed, or when we saw? He said, "Salvation is for you and your house as it says in the Word." Then we stopped praying and received their salvation by faith. In other words, we decided to believe when we prayed. Praise the Lord, it worked. Both of our parents were born again in about six weeks.

God in His wisdom doesn't give us everything we ask for at the drop of a hat. If you take small children into a toy store, they will ask for everything that catches their eyes. If you were foolish enough to purchase everything they desired, not only would you soon be broke, but your house would be full of discarded toys. Most of them would no longer hold interest for the child. On the other hand, if a child sets his heart on one thing and keeps on asking and hoping and keeps on believing over a lengthy period of time, you usually respond, because you know that this is not just a whim. God treats us the same way. So many people do not receive, because it was just a whim with them and they were not really prepared to hang in there. They were not ready to have the same attitude that Jacob had when he wrestled with the angel. *". . . I will not let You go unless You bless me!"* **(Gen. 32:26).** He had to stay wrestling all night to receive.

Remember prayer is not the end, but the means to the end. People have often said, "We have had a wonderful prayer meeting," but the result has been disappointing. Prayer is a two-way conversation. If we do all the talking then God is not able to get a word in. We go away feeling satisfied, but without answers or solutions to our problems. That is religious soul praying, and not Spirit-led, anointed communion.

31

Dealing With Prejudice

One other hindrance to receiving a fresh anointing is religious or denominational prejudice. God often brings a fresh move or revival to the most unusual places or people. The local Baptist pastor or Methodist minister receives the Baptism and starts having Holy Spirit renewal meetings at his church. God begins to move, many people come and are revived, touched by the Spirit and healed. The Pentecostal pastor plays it down by saying, "The Baptist pastor is a novice in the things of the Spirit, so what is going on at his church is irrelevant to our needs." So instead of going to the meetings and receiving a blessing, he and his congregation stay away and pray for revival for their own church. Pride can so easily stop us from receiving, because God is using a beginner.

When the Holy Spirit zapped Gary Folds, the pastor of the Second Baptist church in our hometown, he started having Saturday night renewal meetings. We could have said, "He doesn't know anything, we could do better meetings and have a greater anointing than he, with all our experience." But the Lord enabled us to meet him. Since then we have participated in and have supported his meetings. We have been able to encourage him, share some insights as he felt his way through this new experience. His meetings have increased in anointing, and could be on the way to being a great outpouring of God's Spirit. (As of August 1996 they are in their 81st week of renewal.) We even ended up publishing a book of his testimony called *Bull in a China Shop.*

The media asked John Arnott why God chose the insignificant Airport Vineyard in Toronto to pour out His Spirit on thousands of people coming from all over the world? Instead of giving some deep spiritual answer, John said, "Well, I guess because we are close to the airport." Before the revival, thousands did not come to hear John Arnott preach. He was **not** one of the country's greatest preachers, but God chose to use him. *"But God has chosen the foolish things of the world to put to shame the wise, and God has chosen the weak things of the world to put to shame the things which are mighty; and the base things of the world and the things which are despised God has chosen, and the things which **are not [John Arnott]**, to bring to nothing the things that are, that no flesh should glory in His presence"* **(1 Cor. 1:27-29).**

This does not mean that large prestigious churches cannot have a genuine move of the Holy Spirit. It just means that it is more difficult. Favor with God and favor with man are not always the same. In the last chapter, I share some of the opposition and conflicts that pastors will have with other leaders and people, if and when a renewal hits their church. Remember Jesus said, *"Woe to you when all men speak well of you, For so did their fathers to the false prophets"* **(Luke 6:26).**

33

CHAPTER THREE

Sustaining the Anointing

"Nor do people put new wine into old wineskins, or else the wineskins break, the wine is spilled [and runs out], and the wineskins, are ruined. But they put new wine into new wineskins, and both are preserved" (**Matt. 9:17**). Have you had a genuine move of the Spirit in your church, but it **ran out** after a few days or a few weeks? Unfortunately this happens much too often. In this chapter we will first look at some of the reasons why the anointing is not sustained.

For those of us that are open for a move of God, our desire and God's desire are not always the same. When we ask the Lord God to come and move in our lives or in our church life could we mean, "God move and then move on"? Perhaps we don't want Him to stay, because that would upset our plans and schedules. Maybe we don't mind a short move, a quick blessing, but we want to return to normal as soon as possible. Are we prepared for the long haul? God desires to come and stay among His people. He wants us to trust the Holy Spirit to have control and do unusual acts, as He sees fit. He is not concerned with time, decorum, protocol, tradition, or man's opinions. That comes hard to the flesh, even our religious flesh. We are comfortable with being in control of our lives and our time. We want to know how long meetings will last, what will happen, and what is planned. Unfortunately that is the way to miss God. Jesus (when speaking to Nicodemus) said, *"The wind blows where it wishes, and you hear the sound of it, but cannot tell where it comes from and where it goes. So is everyone who is born of the Spirit"* **(John 3:8).**

Christians are supposed to be unpredictable, not unreliable or irresponsible. Do we want to live rather boring predictable lives, where we know everything that is going to happen by the clock and by routine? Are we living in a rut (which is really a shallow grave)? If we Christians are predictable, then our coming together will also be very predictable and boring. But if we are possessed of the Spirit, then when we come together our meetings will be like that wind. There will be excitement, because God is present and anything is likely to happen. Wonderful miracles will probably take place, and one thing is sure, the meetings will never be boring.

Some pastors become anxious if they can't bring their church back to normal after a move of the Spirit. After all, they need to resume their series of sermons and they need to get back on an even keel. It was fun while it lasted and we will just incorporate the blessing into the system. New wine — old wineskins? The Holy Spirit is not interested in injecting life into an old dead system. He certainly doesn't want to prop up something that is dying. He does not supply a mechanical life support system to a body that is brain dead. He supplies new life. What was okay in grandad's day may not be any good for today.

How many churches have experienced their youth or children coming back from a camp with glowing reports on how God met them in a wonderful way? Youngsters who were cold and indifferent to the things of God have suddenly become fired up. Sunday evening service is devoted to a special youth testimony time. Everyone attending politely applauds, as the youth share their glowing accounts of how God has touched them. Yet two or three weeks later, most, if not all, are back where they were before the camp; cold, cynical, and indifferent. Why is this? Because we did not change the wineskins and allow the youngsters to function and become a viable part of the church's vision. Unless the anointing on those youth is taken seriously and developed, it will fade away. We cannot expect long-lasting revival without changing our wineskins or making a paradigm shift.

A few years ago Kathie and I were ministering in a meeting in Michigan. The church was very well organized. The deacons were trained in hospitality. They parked our car, carried our Bibles, made sure we had refreshments before and after we preached, and supplied drinks and mints at the podium. When the Holy Spirit began to move all of their good intentions went out the window. They were on the floor with the others doing carpet time. The pastor was standing back weeping. Kathie asked, "What is the matter?" He answered, "I've lost control of the meeting." "Don't worry! The Holy Spirit is in control now. He knows what He is doing," she replied.

Continually Drinking

It is not enough for us to have just one filling. I often ask the children, "What would you do if your mother said that the drink she just gave you would have to last for the next three years?" We cannot rely on old anointings, or yesterday's manna to take us through. Just because I was baptized in the Spirit in 1969 or even three weeks ago, doesn't mean I don't need a fresh filling today. *". . . but be filled with the Spirit"* **(Eph. 5:18).** This is not an option, but a command. The original meaning is **not** to be filled with the Spirit just one time, but being continually filled with the Spirit on a daily basis.

One of the results of being filled is *"speaking to one another in psalms and hymns and spiritual songs, singing and making melody in your heart to the Lord"* **(Eph. 5:19).** This is more than a church song service on Sunday morning. Look around at the typical church service, even in Charismatic or Pentecostal churches, you will find large numbers of people including the children and youth who are **not** entering into the praise and worship, yet many of them claim to be spirit-filled. Are we in danger of being spirit-filled by tradition rather than by experience?

What happens after we have been filled with the Spirit? Is that the final goal? We previously saw some of the results of being filled with the Spirit according to **Ephesians 5:19.** We are also told in **Acts 1:8** that we receive power when the Holy Spirit comes upon us, which will enable us to be effective witnesses for the Lord. Our witness to the world must be far more than people seeing us dressed in our Sunday best, our Bibles tucked under our arms, marching off to our weekly church service. I don't believe that was what **Acts 1:8** was about. Christianity is not a religious show that we put on once a week, it is a "supernatural life." *"If we live in the [anointing] Spirit, let us also walk in the [anointing] Spirit"* **(Gal. 5:25).** If the Spirit life is the anointed life, then this must **not** be an experience that just comes and goes. I often tell young folk that if they claim to be saved and Spirit-filled, then there **must** be signs of life and growth.

When a baby is born, then it will breathe, cry, desire food, and respond to its mother. If it is healthy, it will begin to grow, and desire to accomplish more and more. Babies naturally learn and are soon able to sit up and turn over by themselves. A little later they begin to crawl and eventually they start to walk. What is true in the natural is also true in the spiritual.

Religious demons will keep us locked into a system that will keep us from growing. We may receive more theology and more doctrine, but we will be deprived of the power, the freedom, and the joy of the Holy Spirit. We will occasionally be given a few crumbs to sustain us in the wilderness, but we will never enter into the promised land. In fact, those religious spirits will tell us that there is no promised land this side of heaven, and blessing, prosperity, health, joy, laughter, healing, and deliverance are not part and parcel of the gospel. Those demons will tell us that kind of a gospel is a false one. We will be told that the true gospel offers us sickness, hardship, struggle, conflict, and rejection. The problem is that part of what they say is true, in that we do encounter things in life that are not easy situations, but without the blessings, joy and the freedom of the Holy Spirit in our lives, we will never be able to face the conflicts with victory. We will never be able to endure hardness, fight off sickness, defeat poverty, and set the captives free.

"And He was handed the book of the prophet Isaiah. And when He had opened the book, He found the place where it was written: 'The Spirit of the Lord is upon Me, Because He has anointed Me to preach the gospel to the poor. He has sent Me to heal the brokenhearted, To preach deliverance to the captives And recovery of sight to the blind, To set at liberty those who are oppressed, To preach the acceptable year of the Lord'" **(Luke 4:17-19).** The next verses say that everyone's eyes were upon Him after He had read those Scriptures. Then he said *". . . Today this Scripture is fulfilled in your hearing"* **(Luke 4:21).**

One would have thought that there would have been much rejoicing in the synagogue after hearing the wonderful news from Jesus's lips, but it was not to be! Three things happened that made the people mad.

First He said "today," not tomorrow, or yesterday, but **today.** Dead religion will always put the supernatural and revival either in the past or in the future. Some will say, "We don't believe miracles and gifts of healing are for today. They were around in Bible days, but not now. They were just to get the church started." Others will say, "The revival that many are claiming is happening today is spurious. It is full of flaws. The healings are not genuine. We are waiting for a true revival that will come someday, and it will fit our brand of theology."

40

The second thing that made them mad was that He was Joseph's son. "Who does He think He is? He hasn't been awarded a degree in theology. He is not recognized by the leading seminaries. He is not one of our national leaders. He must be a false prophet."

The third thing that filled them with anger was that He insulted them by bringing judgement upon their reaction to Him. He showed them their stubborn, hard, unbelieving hearts. They thought their religious pedigree counted for something and He reminded them that only one widow and one leper received God's blessing. **(See Luke 4:22-29.)** *"So the last will be first, and the first last. For many are called, but few chosen"* **(Matt. 20:16).**

To return to Jesus's fulfillment of **Isaiah 61:1-2**, He did not sympathize with people who were sick, demonized or spiritually oppressed, He healed and delivered them. He did not set up counseling services. He used the **anointing** to break lifetime bondages over them. What a glorious gospel! We believe He has anointed His bride to do the same. He certainly will not anoint religious, skeptical, unbelieving Pharisees. *"Those who are unspiritual do not receive the gifts of God's Spirit, for they are foolishness to them, and they are unable to understand them because they are spiritually discerned"* **(1 Cor. 2:14, NRSV).**

Unfortunately, there are many folk around today who still operate in strong religious traditions. Not only do we have to deal with the skeptics of the world, but we also have to contend with the skeptics in the church. Not only from the **liberals**, but many in the evangelical segment of the church. We don't need self-appointed heresy hunters who think they know it all, and try to belittle and malign anyone who does not subscribe to their narrow, cramped, dead, theological viewpoint.

There is an interesting article in Issue 47, Vol. XIV, No. 3, of *Christian History* magazine. The title of the article is "The Natural, Supernatural." It is an interview with Gordon Fee, who is a professor of New Testament at Regent College in Vancouver, B.C., regarding his book *God's Empowering Presence: The Holy Spirit in the Letters of Paul* (Hendrickson, 1994). During this interview, Gordon Fee conveyed that the Apostle Paul was a Spirit-filled, tongue-talking Christian who practiced divine healing and deliverance, and the churches he visited and wrote to experienced the same. The following questions were then put to Professor Fee.

"Why are some modern Christians reluctant to embrace this aspect of Paul's life and teaching?" Fee responded, "As products of the reformation, we are also products of the Enlightenment. Many of my fellow evangelicals are rationalistic in their approach to Christian faith — we love God with our minds, and we often neglect loving God with our hearts; we don't have a full experience of God's Spirit. We're afraid to experience the Spirit."

Gordon Fee goes on to respond to another question: "What would Paul and the early church then think of the 'holy laughter' in some churches today?" "That sort of thing was not common in the first century, and I'm cautious about speaking of phenomena I've not experienced or witnessed. But my guess is that the early church would see it as a work of the Spirit — whether it's a human response to the Spirit's triggering, or the Spirit Himself who produces the laughter. Laughter is certainly **something** the Spirit could produce."

If most Christians do not have a problem with people crying when the Holy Spirit brings conviction, why should we have a problem with people laughing when the Holy Spirit brings joy?

Pastor Ken Gott of the Sunderland Christian Center in England (which has been experiencing a renewal for almost two years), on page 164 of his book, *The Sunderland Refreshing*, gives a number of scriptural references to laughter. *"To console those who mourn in Zion, To give them beauty for ashes, The oil of joy for mourning, The garment of praise for the spirit of heaviness . . ."* **(Isa. 61:3)**. *". . . Do not be afraid, for behold, I bring you good tidings of great joy which will be to all people"* **(Luke 2:10)**. He mentions that British surgeries are crowded with patients with depression, meaning we could all do with a dose of holy laughter. *"Blessed are you who weep now, For you shall laugh"* **(Luke 6:21)**. *". . . You rejoice with joy inexpressible and full of glory"* **(1 Peter 1:8)**.

Ralph Mahoney, President of World Map, stated in the July/August 1996 issue of *World Map Digest* that apart from a few exceptions, theologians almost never know what God is doing. "They try to understand God by their intellectual abilities — and seldom have any insights given by the Spirit. It seems to me that most labor under the culpability described by Paul, *'Having their understanding darkened . . . because of the ignorance that is in them, because of the hardening [or blindness] of their heart'"* **(Eph. 4:18).**

Back in the early seventies we were part of the house church movement in England. We had been enjoying many months of revival and blessing from the Lord. In one of our meetings, we began to feel that we were getting a little too much blessing and not enough rebuke and correction. We asked the Lord to give us a spirit of repentance, expecting to experience great sorrow for our sins. This must have been our religious minds working, because instead of experiencing a time of weeping, the spirit of joy came upon us and for hours we were on the floor, helplessly laughing before the Lord. Obviously God knew our needs better than we did!

Another time, around 1989, we were preaching in a church in the U.S. We had just finished the message and we were praying for the Holy Spirit to minister. It was a fairly small church of about 150 people. Both of the aisles were full. Suddenly people on the right aisle began to weep and people on the left aisle began to laugh. As we moved across the platform to pray for people, we were affected in the same way. As we stood on the right end of the platform we began weeping, when we moved over to the left we began to laugh. It was a strange experience, but God did some wonderful things that night, meeting the needs of everyone.

Many religious people are having a problem with what they would call "weird manifestations," such as falling down, laughing, shaking, crying, roaring, etc. "This can't be God," they say, "it must be the devil." Yet Jesus, the Son of God, performed things

44

that were far more strange than those just mentioned. On one occasion a deaf and dumb man came to Jesus and He put His fingers into the man's ears and spat on the man's tongue. **(See Mark 7:32-33.)** "How disgusting," one might say. "That is certainly not scriptural." I don't understand the significance of verses 32 and 33, but verses 34 and 35 show the results. Let the theologians or the heresy hunters tell us why it was necessary for Jesus to spit — if they can.

Another account is where Jesus spat in a man's eyes and then asked him if he could see. **(See Mark 8:23.)** Well, of course he couldn't, his eyes were full of spit, and that's probably why he said *". . . I see men like trees, walking. Then He put His hands on his eyes again [**probably wiping the spit out of them**] and made him look up. And he was restored and saw everyone clearly"* **(Mark 8:24-25).**

One other seemingly weird and ridiculous situation is when Jesus spat in the mud, made mud balls, shoved them in a blind man's eyes and then told him to go and wash his face. **(See John 9:6-7.)** The blind man may have thought, "He made my face dirty, now He tells me to wash it? How weird can you get?" But he obeyed and the result was that he was healed. If you read the rest of the story, the religious leaders had a fit over the whole episode. Instead of rejoicing over the miracle, they strained at their religious gnats. The whole story would be quite hilarious, if it were not so pathetic. In the account of the blind man testifying to his denominational leaders, it caused a division amongst them. **(See John 9:16.)** That is why many churches reject the supernatural and the move of the Spirit, because they fear it will cause division in their church, and it probably will. We see from these biblical accounts it is not the strange and weird things that Jesus did that we should be concerned about, but the result — they were all healed.

So, when we see or hear of these strange manifestations in these renewal meetings, let's not attempt to discern with our intellects, but wait to see what the results are. It seems to me that in most cases the results have been very positive. People have been saved, restored, healed, delivered, encouraged, and renewed with a love and a passion to serve the Lord. If the Assembly of God Church in Brownsville, Pensacola, Florida, has had over 30,000 first-time professed conversions in fourteen months or so, then let us give God the glory and stop being suspicious.

The Brownsville Assemblies pastor, John Kilpatrick, in his book, *Feast of Fire*, mentions on page 117 the struggle pastors will have with their reputation, if revival hits their church. People will accuse the pastor of allowing crazy and weird things to go on in his church. It may even come to having to sacrifice his reputation.

Of course the pastor must prepare for the controversial news that **will** be broadcast around his area by the religious folk, and if he overcomes that problem and the revival continues to grow, he may also have to face criticism from religious leaders around the country. We trust he will not fold under the pressure and be tempted to shut it down, thus not being able to sustain the anointing.

Another reason that the anointing is not always sustained is fear of excess. We like to be moderate, and are frightened of excess or going overboard. Not only will this stop churches from receiving the anointing, but it will hinder them from sustaining the anointing. When people fall in love, or are totally dedicated to a cause, or have a passion about something or someone, their behavior is regarded by the average person to be in excess or too radical. My daughter, Faith, is engaged to a young man and because of the ministry they spend a lot of time together. But I noticed that when the young man, David, goes home for a day or two, they call each other about every hour! In the spiritual realm, God will never be satisfied and our spirits will never be satisfied with average Christianity. **Average** commitment, dedication, involvement, and passion, will never touch the heart of God or turn the world upside down.

It is very easy for us to quench the Spirit in our effort to control what we consider to be excessive. *"Do not quench the Spirit"* **(1 Thess. 5:19).** Bible teacher Bob Mumford once told of a church that was praying for revival. Suddenly in the service the power of God hit a middle-aged lady in the congregation. She began to get very emotional, crying out loudly, "Oh! Jesus! Oh! Jesus! Thank You, Jesus! I love You, Jesus!" Immediately two church deacons came to where she was sitting and speedily escorted her out of the service. He said it was the quickest revival he had ever experienced, it started and finished in about two minutes.

Pastors can quench the Holy Spirit by grabbing back control of the meeting when they fear they are no longer in charge. The

Holy Spirit has at times been cut off because leaders have been concerned about the clock. Where there are two or three services on a Sunday morning, time can be very important. If the meeting is going on after the allotted time, others are waiting to come in. Parking problems arise and people become upset. What is a pastor to do? There are no easy answers. Most pastors delegate a special night, or the last morning service, for the Spirit to move. If the Holy Spirit breaks into every service, then the pastor will have some wonderful problems.

I remember hearing a story of an evangelist who made an altar call in this church and two youngsters responded by making their way to the front. They were accosted by two deacons who told them to return to their seats as they were too young to understand what they were doing. How tragic! We must never jump up and stop something, just because it's new to us and we haven't experienced it before. Just because something happens that doesn't fit into our tradition, that doesn't mean it's not from God.

On the other hand, we must not grieve the Holy Spirit and fail to discern that which is of the Lord and that which is not. *"And do not grieve the Holy Spirit of God, by whom you were sealed for the day of redemption"* **(Eph. 4:30).** The Spirit of God can be grieved if people decide to walk out to the rest rooms during a prophetic message, or when a Word of Knowledge is being given out. If children are allowed to play or mess around, if people talk or play with babies during a very sensitive part of the meeting, the Holy Spirit will not compete with our carnality, but will withdraw. Just because children are cute doesn't mean that they should not be trained to be respectful to the Holy Spirit. Some healing evangelists will not allow children to be in their meetings. They arrange a place where the kids can have fun and games while the adults experience the power of the Spirit being ministered to them. In my meetings I always include the children and teach them to pay attention and be sensitive to the Holy Spirit's presence. I also show parents and teachers how to raise the children and teens to hunger for the reality of God.

One of the gifts of the Spirit is the *"Discerning of spirits"* **(1 Cor. 12:10).** This gift enables the recipient to discern between **human** activity, **demonic** activity, and **Holy Spirit** activity. If we are unskilled in this area, we will be in danger of making the following false assumptions depending upon our particular bias:

1. **Misunderstanding true demonic activity.**
   Trying to cast demons out of fleshly emotions.

2. **Not believing in demonic activity.**
   Thinking a person's problem is lack of discipline or some emotional or chemical imbalance, instead of realizing that they are under demonic influence.

3. **Sinning against the Holy Spirit.**
   Crediting the work of the Holy Spirit to demons.

We have shown how the Spirit can be quenched and grieved in our corporate gatherings. We must remember that our meeting together is a product of who we are as individuals. If we quench and grieve the Holy Spirit in our personal lives, then sooner or later it will show up in our church gatherings. Where there is a lack of a genuine relationship with the Lord on a personal level, our coming together will lack the authenticity of a genuine move of God. At best it will be a show, a performance, with lots of hype, but little substance, and at worst it will be dead tradition and formalism.

We need God's presence and anointing in our homes as well as in our churches. During a move of God in the early seventies in England, we visited communities of Christians. As we entered their homes, praise, worship, prayer, and ministry seemed to be going on continually. Even the meal tables were a spiritual experience. Often they would thank the Lord for the food, get carried up in the Spirit and 45 minutes later we were ready to eat. When it was time to wash the dishes (none had dishwashers) everyone had a time of worship around the kitchen sink. When they came together in their corporate gatherings it was just an overflow of what was going on in their homes. What a wonderful way of sustaining the anointing!

CHAPTER FOUR

Bringing the Anointing

For many years the evangelical churches have majored on bringing "the word" to their congregations. Even Pentecostal and Charismatic churches have often only paid lip service to the Holy Spirit. It must be an indictment to Spirit-filled churches when thousands of their members are having to go to other places to receive a fresh touch from the Lord. Not only have we been unable to sustain the anointing from the past, but we don't seem to know how to bring an anointing for today. We have been "business as usual" churches. We have become so bogged down with programs, ministry, counseling, and making the wheels go round that we haven't had the time to seek the presence of the Holy Spirit. The result of this has been "burn out." We have many Pentecostal and Charismatic churches who have become so used to the mundane, that they are rejecting a fresh move of God, even when it is offered to them.

Some time ago I was speaking at a National Children's Pastor's conference. In one of the sessions, I was asked by some children's pastors if it was possible to have a move of God among the children without anyone knowing. I had been sharing on how to bring the anointing to the children and youth. They were concerned that if it happened in their church, when the elders and parents found out, they would not approve. It is impossible to have a corporate move of God without anyone knowing about it. Even a personal move of God upon an individual will be noticed by others, because of the change they will see.

We see the ministry of the Spirit contrasted with the ministry of the law in **2 Corinthians 3:1-18.** Moses had been on the mountain in the presence of God. When he came down with the Ten Commandments (which could not bring life) his face was covered with God's glory. He even had to put a veil over his face, because the glory was too much for the children of Israel to look upon. If the ministry of the law was that glorious, how much more shall the ministry of the Spirit be! **(See verses 7-8.)** We are now called to be ministers of the new covenant which is the ministry of the Spirit. **(See verse 6.)** Bringing the presence of the Holy Spirit to the people does entail a revelation of that passage of Scripture.

Let's no longer depend on teaching and preaching alone, but realize the Holy Spirit's function is to make doctrine become a reality. I have said this on many occasions, "All doctrine is to be experienced, and not merely acquiesced." We have touched on this a little in the first chapter. *". . . By the mouth of two or three witnesses every word shall be established"* **(2 Cor. 13:1).**

The above Scripture is mentioned six times, twice in the Old Testament and four times in the New Testament. Jesus was challenged with that Scripture by the Pharisees. *"The Pharisees there-fore said to Him, 'You bear witness of Yourself; Your witness is not true'"* **(John 8:13)**. *"I am One who bears witness of Myself, and the Father who sent Me bears witness of Me"* **(John 8:18)**. Jesus Himself had previously said, *"If I bear wit-ness of Myself, My witness is not true. There is another [**His Father and also the Holy Spirit in John**] who bears witness of Me, and I know that the witness which He witnesses of Me is true"* **(John 5:31-32)**.

The Father bore witness to Jesus by anointing Him. He did not merely bear witness to His ministry, but to Him. As a Son, He was constantly anointed. We may have our ministry anointed, but we can so often fall back into the flesh in our daily walk. That is one of the main differences between our walk and Christ's.

In law, to establish the validity of what has been said, we need a reliable witness. In the spiritual realm, to establish the validity of our preaching, we need the confirmation or witness of the Holy Spirit. So often we have not experienced a move of God, be-cause we have been satisfied with just one witness: the witness of the Word. But we need a second witness, even the Spirit of Truth which will bring the anointing upon the word preached. This will change it from a Logos word to a Rhema word. Yet better still, a third witness. That is when the Holy Spirit not only bears witness to the word preached, but also bears witness with our Spirit. *"The Spirit Himself bears witness with our spirit that we are chil-dren of God"* **(Rom. 8:16)**. This is how God by His Spirit can do more in a few seconds than we can do in months and years with our feeble, futile, un-anointed preaching and counseling.

From our individual perspective, it is not enough for us to believe and claim **John 3:16.** We also need to be sealed with the Holy Spirit of promise **(see Eph. 1:13),** so that we may **know** that we **know** that we are the children of God. The result being, we cry out Abba! [Daddy] Father! *"For you did not receive the spirit of bondage again to fear, but you received the Spirit of adoption by whom we cry out 'Abba, Father'"* **(Rom. 8:15).**

This is also very important with children. Just because they have learned **John 3:16**, and they claim to believe it, doesn't necessarily make them Christians. They must also **experience** the **Spirit of adoption.**

When we minister in churches we ask for the Holy Spirit to come after the Word has been preached. This is the time to allow the Holy Spirit to do His work. This way the Word is established in the hearts of the hearers. Sometimes it takes time for the breakthrough. We must often wait patiently for the Holy Spirit to do as He wants.

Many people who have read my book *Kids in Combat* have put into practice something that I mentioned in one of the chapters. More than once in meetings I have prayed for numbers of children and youth. I then would sit down, leaving them on the platform looking rather sheepish. Several minutes would pass and nothing would happen. Sometimes I would wait as long as 20 minutes before the Holy Spirit touched the youngsters. As long as I stayed in faith and was obedient to Him, great things would happen. It is very encouraging when the preachers and teachers write or call me saying they have had a mighty move of God by doing the same thing as I did. One person said they nearly gave up as the teens were standing around giggling after she had prayed. She then remembered the chapter and hung in there and after a little time God took hold of them. They ended up being changed in a powerful way as the Spirit moved on them for many hours.

We bring the presence of the Holy Spirit into meetings by faith. *"The mystery which has been hidden from ages and from generations, but now has been revealed to His saints. To them God willed to make known what are the riches of the glory of this mystery among the Gentiles: which is Christ in you, the hope of glory"* (**Col. 1:26-27**). Christ means "The Anointed One." We bring Him, The Anointed One, with us when we minister. As we allow His life to pour forth out of us, then His glory is revealed and sinners are saved, lives are transformed, bodies are healed, and the captives are set free. Any willing, yielded vessel can bring the anointing. We don't always have to wait for Benny Hinn, Randy Clark, or Rodney Howard-Browne to come to town before God can move.

Just recently we experienced a move of God upon children and teens at a church in North Carolina. After they received the Baptism of the Holy Spirit and the gift of tongues, I sent them out to pray for the adult congregation. I told them that they may be just clay pots and some of them may be cracked pots, but God wanted to use them. *"But we have this treasure in earthen vessels, that the excellence of the power may be of God and not of us"* (**2 Cor. 4:7**).

Many wonderful things happened that night. One man took off his knee brace and hopped on one leg, claiming he was healed. A lady took off her back brace, waved her arms in the air testifying that she was healed. Another lady who said that she was due for surgery on her wrist and elbow was experiencing healing, as all the pain and stiffness disappeared. A little five-year-old boy (whose parents thought he had broken his ankle) took off the strapping and ran around with no pain. Another man said a seven or eight year old prophesied over him and read his mail. One little girl said she prayed for 18 people and many of them were still on the floor, being dealt with by the Lord.

Bringing the anointing is not as difficult as our religious minds would try to tell us. In fact, it's easy and fun to have meetings when the Holy Spirit is allowed to have His way. He sets us free from striving and struggling and puts us in a place of rest. We can watch in amazement as we see how good He is at doing what He knows best. God responds to our faith, so remember faith is an important key in bringing the anointing.

Another key is not to allow the spirit of the world or religious spirits to bind us up and control us. Satan is going to oppose the moving of the Spirit. Foolishness, mocking, playing around, is something that happens with carnal children and youth. It's the spirit of the world, coming into the church, but we can defeat that spirit. We must remember, *". . . Because He who is in you is greater than he who is in the world"* (**1 John 4:4**).

As mentioned in the previous chapter, we must be careful about people grieving the Holy Spirit. Not only will it stop the

Spirit from being sustained, it will also stop Him from coming. Being insensitive will grieve Him, and make Him depart. Katherine Khulman, the great healing evangelist, said during one of her meetings, "Please don't grieve the Holy Spirit, He is all that I have." Perhaps that is why many of us have been unable to bring the anointing in our churches, because we have not seen our desperate need of Him.

When I am praying for the Holy Spirit to come, I tell children to remember that He is like a dove. A dove is a bird and if you want a bird to come near, you have to be very still. When I lived in England, I worked in London. Sometimes during my lunch hour I would go into a small park in the city called Lincoln-in-Fields. The sparrows were so tame that they would fly onto your hand, if you had food for them. The secret was that you had to be very quiet and still.

Children have a habit of talking, poking, distracting each other, and jumping around, etc. Although this is permissible during playtime, it is not during **pray** time. When they become quiet and reverent, the Holy Spirit descends. This is true for all of us. You cannot bring the Holy Spirit where there is no desire to receive Him. Where there is no demand, there is no supply. If there were no demand for drugs today, they would not be brought to the streets or the marketplace. The drug lords would go out of business. What is true with the negative is also true with the positive. Even Jesus Himself could **not** do much in one place, because of the unbelief of the people. *"And He did not do many mighty works there because of their unbelief"* (**Matt. 13:58**).

The reason the Holy Spirit descended upon the 120 in the upper room on the day of Pentecost is that they were all of one mind. We can gather people together in one place, but if we are all of different minds with different agendas, all doing our own thing, then we will grieve the Holy Spirit and He will retreat.

When you bring the anointing, religious spirits may rise up in people and oppose it. Do not let them intimidate you. The anointing is there to break the yoke and that includes religious strongholds. *". . . And the yoke will be destroyed because of the anointing oil"* **(Isa. 10:27).** Remember the warning of Jesus not to cast your pearls before swine. We don't want to force the anointing on people, when they need time to adjust. We must also be willing to shake off the dust from our feet **(Matt. 10:14),** when religious spirits have control in a church and the people are not willing to give them up. There are plenty of other people around who are hungry for a mighty move of God.

Unfortunately there are numbers of pastors who have been in the tradition of Pentecost for years. They have seen it all before. Nothing seems to move them. They have become rather cynical, and now they can neither receive or bring a move of the Spirit. The disappointments of the past, seeing flaky manifestations and false healings, deliverances where people shook, rolled and rattled, but their lives did not change, has made them become overcautious and suspicious of any moving of the Spirit.

Unbelief and skepticism is an awful thing. Some seven years ago we were ministering in a church in North Carolina. We were introduced to another pastor who was open for us to come and minister in his church. We went to his house to meet him and his elders. We shared our vision about children and showed him our promotional video. On the video are live scenes of children praying for other children and adults. As the children were praying, many were being slain or falling out in the Spirit. After seeing the video, the pastor said, "I have seen this falling down before. We had it in our church years ago, but it did not produce any lasting fruit. I am not impressed." Where other people had been brought to tears by seeing the video, and many churches have had revival just by watching it and letting their children see what God can do through them, he did not respond.

Early in 1996, I was preaching at a church in the same state. After the weekend the pastor was so excited he said, "I want the churches that we are connected with to have you come to them." He then named a number of pastors that they relate to, including the pastor who saw the video some years ago. "Oh, he would **not** want us to come," I said. "He doesn't like all this kind of Holy Spirit stuff." "Don't you believe it, he loves it," he replied. "Well, he never used to," I said. "That was before he went to the Toronto Airport Church. He is changed." The pastor went on to tell me how free and excited that other pastor now is. He finally received a fresh touch.

IF:

1. Pastors are willing to humble themselves.

2. Stop taking control.

3. Not allow the past to make them cynical.

4. Not become intimidated by religious people in their church, or other local pastors in their denomination.

5. Get into faith and be ready for a fresh touch. **Then,** the following will happen:

   A. God will move on them and their church.

   B. God will make them an instrument to bring to the anointing.

CHAPTER FIVE

Imparting the Anointing

After bringing the anointing, we need to be able to **impart** the anointing. **Bringing** the anointing into a meeting makes available the presence of the Holy Spirit to all. **Imparting** the anointing is not only making the anointing available to others, but it enables us to be a conduit for the Holy Spirit to flow through and to touch others. We become the vessel which God uses. In the story of the lame man begging alms at the temple gate, Peter imparted healing to him. *"Then Peter said, 'Silver and gold I do not have, but what I do have I give you: In the name of Jesus Christ of Nazareth, rise up and walk'"* (**Acts 3:6**). He did not pray for the man, and he did not pray with the man for healing, but he imparted the healing power of God to him. Imparting the anointing is one step further than praying for God to do something. We can and should beseech God on the behalf of others, but we can, as the anointing comes upon us, impart it.

Often we lay hands on people and pray for them, yet I believe that the gospel account in Mark means more than praying for them. *" . . . They will lay hands on the sick, and they will recover"* (**Mark 16:18**). It is not saying that we pray and ask the Lord in faith to heal them, but instead we are to impart the healing. There is, of course, a verse which encourages the elders to pray for the sick. *"Is anyone among you sick? Let him call for the elders of the church, and let them pray over him, anointing him with oil in the name of the Lord. And the prayer of faith will save the sick, and the Lord will raise him up . . ."* (**James 5:14-15**). Both kinds of ministry are acceptable, but here we are talking about **impartation.**

When the Lord blesses, He often does many different things. The anointing to bring the Baptism of the Spirit, or to heal or deliver can be received in a number of different ways.

1. Healing or miracles by using our faith. When we operate our ministry, using our faith, God honors it and the person in need will receive the blessing. *"Now when He had said these things, He cried with a loud voice, 'Lazarus, come forth!'"* (**John 11:43**). Lazarus did not have the faith to be raised from the dead, but Jesus did!

2. Healing or blessing by ours and recipient's faith. We discern that the person needing prayer has the faith to receive their blessing, so we pray in faith knowing that they will respond to the anointing. *"And when He had come into the house, the blind men came to Him. And Jesus said to them, 'Do you believe that I am able to do this?' They said to Him, 'Yes, Lord.' Then He touched their eyes, saying, 'According to your faith let it be to you.' And their eyes were opened . . ."* (**Matt. 9:28-30**).

3. Healing or blessing comes in spite of us. The person may have the faith to receive for themselves, even when we may not feel as though we have much faith or anointing to pray with results. Or in our religious mind-set, we may not regard the person as worthy or qualified to receive. There are many times when we act in obedience, regardless of our feelings, and this is when God often surprises us. *"While Peter was still speaking these words, the Holy Spirit fell upon all those who heard the word. And those of the circumcision who believed were astonished, as many as came with Peter, because the gift of the Holy Spirit had been poured out on the Gentiles also. For they heard them speak with tongues and magnify God . . . "*(**Acts 10:44-46**). When God poured the Holy Spirit on the Catholics in the sixties and seventies, most mainline Pentecostals had a problem with accepting that as a genuine outpouring. Man often judges by what he considers to be correct doctrine.

In other words, they believe that God will only bless those that are doctrinally sound, but sometimes God blesses hungry hearts and reveals doctrine to them later.

My father, who was Jewish, was saved in his sleep. During the night he sat up in bed, raised his hands and cried out, "Jesus, my Messiah." Two weeks later he went forward at a crusade and accepted Christ. God supernaturally touched his heart and spirit first, then through the preaching of the Gospel, he comprehended the doctrine of salvation with his mind.

4. Healing or blessing comes through the combined faith of the people. The person we pray for receives because of the combined faith of the people present. The centurion had faith for Jesus to speak the word of faith to heal his servant. Jesus had the faith because He responded to the centurion's request and the servant was healed. **(See Matt. 8:8.)** *"Again I say to you that if two of you agree on earth concerning anything that they ask, it will be done for them by My Father in heaven"* **(Matt. 18:19).**

5. Divine impartation. There are times when we can sense a divine impartation flowing out of us. As we lay hands or speak the word, the person receives what the Lord has for them. Jesus imparted the Holy Spirit to the disciples by breathing on them. *"And when He had said this, He breathed on them, and said to them, 'Receive the Holy Spirit'"* **(John 20:22).**

There was a time when Jesus merely spoke the word and healing took place. *"The centurion answered and said, 'Lord, I am not worthy that You should come under my roof. But only speak a word, and my servant will be healed'"* **(Matt. 8:8).** In the book of Acts *". . . Stephen, full of faith and power, did great wonders and signs among the people"* **(Acts 6:8).** Ananias laid hands on Paul to receive the Holy Spirit and receive his sight. Notice he did not pray for Paul. *" . . . And Ananias went his way and entered the house; and laying his hands on him he said, 'Brother Saul, the Lord Jesus, who appeared to you on the road as you came, has sent me that you may receive your sight and be filled with the Holy Spirit"* **(Acts 9:17).**

There are also a number of accounts of Paul imparting the anointing. **(See Acts 14:8-10, 16:18, 19:6, 19:11-12.)** There is another account of Paul praying, laying on his hands and healing someone. *"And it happened that the father of Publius lay sick of a fever and dysentery. Paul went in to him and prayed, and he laid his hands on him and healed him"* **(Acts 28:8).** It's quite possible that when Paul prayed, before he laid hands on Publius' father, he was praying for the healing anointing, rather than praying for the Lord to heal the man. Notice it says that Paul healed him. We know that all healing comes from God, yet it was His anointing flowing through Paul that actually did the healing.

Let us go back again to when Peter and John went to the temple to pray and they met the lame beggar at the gate. Peter ministered to him in a way that most Christians would not dream of doing. *"Who, seeing Peter and John about to go into the temple, asked for alms. And fixing his eyes on him, with John, Peter said, 'Look at us.' [We **would have said, "Look at Jesus" or "Look to the Lord."]** So he gave them his attention, expecting to receive something from them. Then Peter said, 'Silver and gold I do not have, but what I do have I give you: In the name of Jesus Christ of Nazareth, rise up and walk"* **(Acts 3:3-6).** If we had felt bold we may have invited him to a healing meeting, or if we were especially bold, we probably would have said, "Here are a few dollars and let me pray for you, because the Lord is still healing people today. The difference between Peter and us is that he imparted the anointing and we usually just pray for it. Once we have seen that, we realize that impartation is greater than just praying. But then, there is another way of imparting that doesn't really involve us much.

Many years ago when we first were baptized in the Holy Spirit, we were having meetings in our house in England. We had invited a couple over to a meeting. The girl's mother was a lady-in-waiting to the Queen and the girl's husband was an Anglican Curate (assistant pastor). Needless to say, they were very upper class. We had been having a number of wild meetings and we were concerned that nothing would happen to put them off. In fact, we had prayed and asked the Lord to keep the meeting orderly. During the praise and worship, the Spirit began to fall. A missionary sister, overcome by the Spirit, suddenly took off and flew through the air, landing on her back in another part of the room. Immediately I said, "Oh, Lord, that has messed everything up, this will surely put them off." But they had their eyes closed all the time, so I don't believe they witnessed that strange manifestation. Eventually I asked if anyone wanted to be filled with the Spirit. I offered to pray for them. Immediately the couple jumped up and I began to make my way over to where they stood. I was still several feet from them when suddenly they both fell down on the floor and began speaking in tongues. God had imparted His anointing to them without my assistance.

A few years ago I was at a church in Florida doing a seminar for parents and teachers on ministering to children and youth. At the close of the seminar, I invited teachers and parents to come up for prayer. An Assembly of God children's Sunday School teacher was so overcome by the Holy Spirit after I prayed that a number of us carried her out to her car at the end of the seminar. "You think you can make it home?" I asked. "I believe I can," she said, talking as though she were drunk.

On Sunday night when I had the "miracle service" (using children to pray for the adults), she attended. She stood up and testified what had happened to her. "I have been a Sunday School teacher for 25 years. After my experience of the Holy Spirit at the Saturday seminar, I took my children's class on the Sunday morning. I felt such an anointing on me that I just stood in front of them and said, 'The Spirit of Christ is in me.' I waved my hands across the room and all the children fell down as they were overcome by the Spirit. I never touched them or prompted them. In fact, it has never happened in our church before."

She had become a carrier and a channel for a divine impartation to be released. There are many testimonies available today on tapes and in books, from different people and other ministries that give similar accounts.

Pastor Bo Daniels has a church in Jonesboro, a small town a few miles south of Atlanta, Georgia. Although Pastor Bo had been in the ministry for 50 years (he preached his first sermon at age seven and went full time at nine), he was looking for a fresh touch. In 1995 he and his wife were taking a vacation. They planned to go to the ocean to rest and seek the Lord. He told his congregation that he was coming back in two weeks with something from God and they should be ready to receive it in the Sunday morning service.

On the journey to their vacation spot, they were planning to stop by a friend's church to preach for him. When they called the pastor, he said, "You can't come to preach because we won't be there." "Where will you be?" asked Bo. "We are all going to the revival meetings in New Orleans," he said. "Why don't you come and join us? God is really moving. Rodney Howard-Browne is conducting the meetings." Bo said he would pray about it. After some discussion and prayer, he and his wife decided to go.

He said that when they arrived at the meeting, the presence of the Holy Spirit was very powerful. They just sat in every meeting, soaking up the presence of the Lord. Afterwards he told me that too many pastors come for a quick look and get nothing, because they aren't thirsty enough.

After two or three days he began to receive a fresh filling, and finally at the end of one meeting he was carried to his car because he couldn't walk. Someone noticed Rodney Howard-Browne going to his car. "Brother Rodney! Come and see this pastor, he is so overcome by the Spirit that he can hardly walk." Rodney came over, laid hands on Bo, and began to pray in tongues. Bo received the interpretation himself. The Lord said, "You have been touched by My Spirit and you are anxious to share with your church what I have done for you. But I want this anointing and revelation to have time to go deep into your spirit. Therefore I command you not to talk until further notice."

The next and final night Bo was at the revival meeting. Brother Rodney called him up to testify what the Lord had done for him. Needless to say, he was not allowed to speak, so he wrote it down. Rodney said to him, "Are you scheduled to preach at your church next Sunday?" Bo nodded yes. "I would like to be a fly on the wall," replied Rodney with a laugh.

When Bo checked out of his hotel not speaking, and when he went to a store, people thought he was deaf and dumb, so they shouted and waved their arms at him. Bo arrived back on Sunday at his church. After the praise and worship he got up to preach, but he was still not allowed to speak. As he could say nothing, he just laid hands on the people and laughed. Revival started to break out in his church. For 42 days Bo remained silent, but the church did not fall apart. Many healings, deliverances, and salvations took place during that time.

Kathie and I visited his church several times when he was unable to speak and were blessed by the presence of the Lord. Later, when he was able to preach again, we invited him to come to Macon and testify to our local pastors. Incidentally, he is an excellent preacher.

One of the most spectacular things is to see God touching and moving on people when the minister has little to do with it. Divine impartation comes directly from heaven. There is one thing to have people fall down under conviction in a meeting, but when it also happens to people in their houses a mile or so away, then we are seeing a great outpouring. There are many accounts in history of revivals where that has happened.

Anointed Praise and Worship

It is important that our praise and worship team should not only be able to bring the anointing, but also impart the anointing to the worshipers. Some churches choose a person to be a song leader because they have a good singing voice and some musical talent. This should not be the only criterion. Often the most anointed worship leaders don't have particularly great voices, but they are sensitive to the Spirit of God. If the Spirit of revival is upon the worship team and they allow the anointing to flow out to the congregation, many wonderful miracles can happen during the worship time. It is not enough just to sing the latest songs from the music industry, but to choose the songs the Holy Spirit initiates.

Worship is like the gifts of the Spirit. One doesn't stand up and give out his or her favorite prophecy, or whatever they have been rehearsing. I have heard songs sung for many months after all the anointing has been wrung out of them. It is like hearing the same message over and over again. If we are in tune with the Holy Spirit we will know when to drop a song and when to pick it up, if it should ever be picked up again. We must also be careful of soul ties to certain songs. Just because a tune is pretty and the words sound spiritual doesn't mean it is scriptural. Although there are many great songs being written today, some of them are religious, rather than scriptural. For example, asking God to do what He has already done is not only unbiblical, but it robs us from apprehending His promises for today. Remember we are living in the New Testament covenant, not the Old Testament. The Holy Spirit only bears witness to truth, so the songs that continually put us back in the Old Testament will never be truly anointed. They may generate a lot of soulish, religious sentimentalism, but they will **not** bring forth freedom and lasting deliverance.

When we come together, the Holy Spirit has a theme for us. It is not just a collection of nice songs that we sing, but they must relate to what God is saying. At the end of the meeting, we should know that God has spoken to us. Through the worship and praise, the gifts of the Spirit, testimonies, sharing and the message, often a central theme will emerge. As every joint supplies, so the body is built up. **(See Eph. 4:16.)** As the impartation of the Holy Spirit is given to everyone, then instead of one man exhorting a passive congregation, it's every member exhorting each other. **(See Heb. 10:25.)** The impartation of the anointing is **not** just to bless and heal people, but to make every Christian function, that they become an asset to the Kingdom of God.

Some Pentecostals have a problem with choreographed dancing. They believe that only spontaneous "dancing in the Spirit" is anointed. A well-known Bible teacher once said, "Rehearsed dancing is of the flesh, because if you close your eyes you can't see it." You could apply the same faulty logic to preaching. "If you stop your ears you can't hear the message, so it must be of the flesh. If only spontaneous dancing is in the Spirit, then prepared sermons and rehearsed worship and praise is in the flesh. This belief, of course, is nonsense. I have heard prepared sermons, well rehearsed worship songs, and have seen dances that haven't been anointed and on other occasions they have been. I have also heard and seen spontaneous sermons, songs, worship and dances with the same results. Surely it is not a question of whether a message, a song, or a dance is rehearsed or not, but is it God approved, is it **anointed?**

The Holy Spirit also works through talent, or even lack of it. God can anoint a cracked singing voice and it can minister to you better than the best tenor or soprano, but it must be anointed. A beautiful voice can please people, even if it is **not** anointed, a cracked voice can't.

CHAPTER SIX

Channel the Anointing

Much of the anointing that we experience is like raw electricity, it needs to be harnessed or channeled. It is one thing to fall down, shake, cry, laugh, get goose bumps and feel good, but there are other things that the Holy Spirit wants to do for us and through us. That initial cleansing, which brings conviction and deliverance and restores joy, is a wonderful and necessary experience, but we must go on from there. The Holy Spirit cleans us out and makes us an open channel for Him to flow through to touch other people's lives.

Previously, our prayers may have been weak and ineffective, but the anointing is to turn us into powerful prayer warriors. Our witnessing may have been ineffective or nonexistent, but the anointing will give us the same boldness that the disciples had on the day of Pentecost. *"But you shall receive power when the Holy Spirit has come upon you; and you shall be witnesses to Me . . ."* (Acts 1:8). If we know how to channel the anointing, we will affect those around us.

Kathie and I were preaching in a church one time. We had spent three weeks with the people and the Holy Spirit had been moving powerfully, but something was not quite right. Suddenly the Holy Spirit said, "Quit! I am not going to pour My Spirit out anymore." "Why, Lord?" we said. "Because they want to contain My anointing within the four walls of the church building, and just bless themselves. They aren't willing to be channels to pour out My love and life to the community, because they are too selfish."

The Lord has made available to us nine supernatural gifts. **(See 1 Cor. 12:7-10.)** In fact, at the beginning of chapter 12 Paul says, *"Now concerning spiritual gifts, brethren, I do not want you to be ignorant"* **(1 Cor. 12:1).** Unfortunately large numbers of Christians are ignorant concerning spiritual gifts. The Baptism of the Holy Spirit is to bring us into the realm of operating in spiritual gifts. These gifts are not optional extras, but important tools with which to do a job. *"But earnestly desire the best gifts"* **(1 Cor. 12:31).** *"Therefore, brethren, desire earnestly to prophesy, and do not forbid to speak with tongues"* **(1 Cor. 14:39).**

Of the nine gifts of the Spirit, there are:

Three **inspirational** gifts to enable us to **think** like God.

1. Word of wisdom.
2. Word of knowledge.
3. Discerning of spirits.

Three **verbal** gifts to enable us to **talk** like God.

1. **Prophesy.**
2. **Tongues.**
3. **Interpretation of tongues**.

Three **power** gifts to enable us to **act** like God.

1. **Faith.**
2. **Healing.**
3. **Miracles.**

I wrote a book several years ago called *Equipping the Younger Saints.* In chapter 5, "Explaining Spiritual Gifts," I go into some detail about the gifts and show how children and youth can operate in those gifts in their lives. Some people believe that we should look to see which one of those gifts is for us, as everyone has **one** special gift allocated to them. The ministers who brought us into the realm of the Holy Spirit, taught us that we could use all nine gifts to minister. We did not know any different and so we believed it! We soon found out that we can operate in all the gifts, as the Spirit wills.

Paul made a difference between limiting the use of gifts in a meeting. *"Do all have gifts of healings? Do all speak with tongues? Do all interpret?"* **(1 Cor. 12:30).** And encouraging people to desire for spiritual gifts to operate in their lives. *"For you can all prophesy one by one, that all may learn and all may be encouraged"* **(1 Cor. 14:31).** *"I wish you all spoke with tongues, but even more that you prophesied . . ."* **(1 Cor. 14:5).**

Immature Christians can jump up and try to move in all of the gifts in order to show off or take control of a meeting. Mature believers will focus the gifts in such a way as to edify the Body of Christ. They will wait until the Lord gives them the green light. When they receive a gift, they will discern the timing of it. Is it for now or later? Who is it for, an individual, or for everyone? Is it for public or private hearing, etc? Remember spiritual gifts are of the Holy Spirit. They come from Him and they belong to Him. They are not ours to use whenever we like. We are called to be an open channel for the gifts to flow through to the recipients. Remember, we don't have any spiritual gifts as such, but **if** we have been filled with the Holy Spirit, then all those nine gifts are available to flow through us.

Some of the gifts of the Spirit are **not** just limited to the church meeting, but should be available to use in the marketplace. The word of wisdom, the word of knowledge, miracles and healing were used in the marketplace throughout the New Testament. We have tended to lock up the power of the Holy Spirit within the four walls of the church. It's time we took the anointing into the open.

The gifts of the Spirit should also operate through us as we meet with nonbelievers. Many of us have family, friends, and acquaintances who we see from time to time. Perhaps we have been invited to a family reunion or a birthday or wedding, this is **not** the time to shut down the anointing. The Holy Spirit is not limited in His operation to a church environment. Many of us think that unless we are in an official church building with a pulpit, etc., and we have praise and worship first, we cannot operate spiritually. There is a danger of living our lives in compartments, i.e., religious or spiritual, verses secular. If the Holy Spirit is like the wind, then you cannot control Him or box Him in. If we are truly living all the time in the Spirit, then we are like the wind. **(See John 3:8.)** Let's not shut down the anointing in our lives because of the fear of men. *"The fear of man brings a snare"* **(Prov. 29:25).**

One of the church's commissions is to evangelize. In the past, churches have tried door-to-door witnessing. They have also tried allocating local telephone numbers to their members in order to phone people and invite them to a special event. This program was worked out on a percentage idea. Call 10,000 people and by sheer weight of numbers you must get some converts. Unfortunately, considering the time and effort, the results in most cases were not all that successful. Although one salvation is important to God, He doesn't want us to be wasteful with our resources in our evangelistic efforts. The Holy Spirit is always efficient. Perhaps we have been using some old-fashioned hit-and-miss methods. Bows and arrows, spears and shotguns are no longer capable of bringing the results. We must move with the times. The Holy Spirit is not bound by old-fashioned traditions.

The main reason America won the Gulf War a few years ago was because of the high technology that was implemented through the U.S. Air Force. Laser guided missiles were specially designed to hit the target. If man has progressed so much in the natural realm, then why should he not in the spiritual realm?

The Holy Spirit knows what to target better than we do. Some years ago, an evangelist friend of ours was driving through a street in England. The Lord suddenly spoke to him and said that in a certain house there was a boy that was sick. The Lord then told him to go and pray for the boy. He stopped at the house, got out of his car and knocked on the door. A lady opened the door and he asked her if she had a sick boy in the house. She said, "Yes." Then he said, "I would like to minister to him." Thinking he was a doctor, she took him up to the sick boy's room. He laid hands on the boy, prayed for him, and he was instantly healed. He then led the boy and the mother to the Lord. When the story became known, all the neighbors in the whole street were saved within a few weeks. Sometime later, I had the privilege of preaching in one of the house meetings that they were having. It was wonderful to see all these new converts experiencing the reality of God's healing and saving power.

My wife, Kathie, wrote a book some years ago called *Living in the Supernatural*. In chapter 2, she talks about proving God. On the heading called "Proving God in the Marketplace," I would like to quote some of her testimonies:

"After David and I were married I worked in the accounting department of a company in London. God's Spirit was moving, and many people came to our home fellowship. We knew it was only a matter of time before we went into full-time ministry. I was determined to leave that company with a great testimony.

"The Spirit began to manifest His power in our office, and the people who worked there sensed the reality of the Lord. One of the things that caught the attention of the chief accountant and the staff was how the Lord moved on my behalf at the end of every month when we tried to balance the books. While everyone else was frantically pouring over the huge ledger sheets looking for mistakes to correct, I would bow my head and pray, and the Holy Spirit would immediately tell me the error. Consequently, my books and accounts were balanced within a few minutes.

"At one time there was a mail strike, which was expected to last a couple of weeks. Since we were unable to send out the monthly statements, no one bothered to prepare them for mailing. After a few days, the Holy Spirit told me to get the statements ready, because the strike would be over in the morning. As I folded the statements and put them into envelopes, the assistant accountant asked me what I was doing. 'The Lord told me I can mail them in the morning,' I replied. He just rolled his eyes in disbelief.

"The next day's early morning news reported that the strike was over. I picked up my statements, hurried to the post office and was back by 9:20 a.m. When I returned, the chief accountant asked me if I would help the others prepare their mail."

Kathie goes on to give some other accounts:

"A few weeks later there was an Asian flu epidemic in London. The symptoms lasted two or three weeks. The chief accountant arranged for everyone to get a flu shot, but I declined. 'This flu shot is ninety percent proof,' he angrily told me. 'Well, my protection is one hundred percent proof,' I replied.

"Later that afternoon I began to sneeze, my nose began to run, and my eyes were watering. When it was time to go home, my coworkers called out laughingly, 'See you in a couple of weeks.'

"In the train on the way home I prayed, 'This healing thing was Your idea, so now it's up to You, Lord. I must be fit for tomorrow.' But I felt worse. When I arrived home, I told my husband, David, the situation, and he prayed for me. I was healed instantly. The next morning I arrived at work perfectly healthy, much to the amazement of the staff. Although they knew the Lord had healed me, they didn't want to acknowledge Him.

"Then the Lord added to it with an experience that happened after I left the company. After four months of serving in full-time ministry, I received a phone call from the chief accountant. 'Kathie, we have a mistake somewhere in our sales accounts, and we cannot find it. We have looked and looked, but with no luck. We thought that maybe you could help us find it. You could ask Him — you know, the Man up there — and He will tell you where it is.' My old boss did not want to use the words 'pray' or 'God,' but he was getting close. They were so desperate that he offered to pay me anything I wanted. I knew this would be an excellent opportunity for God to manifest His power, so I agreed to come.

"The next day, as I walked from the train station to the office, I said to the Lord, 'Father! This is a great occasion for You to be glorified. They know that I am going to ask You where the mistake is, so I believe that You will show me right away.'

"When I walked into the office, I found they had placed about two hundred very large ledger sheets full of figures on a desk. It would normally take at least a week to sort through them. The other people sat at their desks, pretending to work, but were watching me out of the corners of their eyes.

"Bowing my head briefly, I prayed, 'Okay, Lord! Now show me.' I turned the sheets one at a time. Suddenly, the Holy Spirit said, 'There in the middle of the page.' I immediately spotted the mistake and showed it to the chief accountant. No more than five minutes had passed since I began looking for the error. Everyone, including my ex-boss, was stunned. As he thanked me, I said, 'Don't thank me. You know I couldn't have done this by myself.'"

"One time I was going to a grocery store where a girl was bagging the groceries in the line next to mine. She was not in a good mood. The Holy Spirit said, 'She is rebelling against someone in authority in her life. Tell her this person only wants what is good for her. I have placed that person in her life.' I began to debate with the Lord. But I have since learned that whenever I do that, I never win! 'Lord, if she comes out the same door as I do, I'll know You want me to talk to her.' Relieved that she went out the other door, I determined to pray for her that night at home.

"As I walked to my car, the Holy Spirit prompted me again, 'I asked you to tell her.' 'If she is on my side of the store when I go back in,' I said, 'I will know that You actually want me to speak to her.' I went back inside, and she went out the opposite door, talking to the customer with her. I was relieved. But as I walked back toward my car, she suddenly headed in my direction. I knew that if I continued to disobey the Holy Spirit, that every time I went back to that store I would remember my unwillingness to follow the Lord's directions.

"I took a deep breath and walked toward her. 'Excuse me,' I said. 'I am a Christian, and I believe the Lord has given me a word for you.' She looked as though she wanted to smack me, but I continued to tell what the Holy Spirit had shown me. Her face changed, and she began to cry right there in the parking lot. 'I am a Christian, too,' she said, 'My youth pastor has been trying so hard to minister to me, but I have rebelled against everything he's tried to do. Tonight at my youth meeting, I will ask him to forgive me.'"

I have shared some of those testimonies of Kathie's to show that the gifts of the Spirit are not to be laid aside, but they are part of our equipment to be used for warfare. Remember we are called to be soldiers. Spiritual warfare is not just relegated to church prayer meetings, but it is operating in the anointing and using the gifts skillfully and effectively. Exercising the gifts, even with mistakes, will eventually bring success.

Some years ago I was doing a family seminar at Christ for the Nations in Dallas, Texas. During one of the sessions, a youth pastor from Kentucky asked me to have lunch with him and his family. I had preached at his church previously. He told me that they had a move of the Spirit recently upon the children. They called the children to the front and began to sing the song "Jesus loves me this I know, for the Bible tells me so," when many of the children were overcome by the Holy Spirit and began to receive visions. One little seven year old by the name of Jessica was really affected. He told me her mother had called him on the phone the next day and said, "What have you done to my daughter?" He replied, "I didn't do anything," "Yes, you did! You laid hands on her," she said. He then heard the little girl in the background say, "No, Mommy, it wasn't him that laid hands on me, it was the man in white." "Oh, my goodness," the mother said. "We were at the shopping mall this morning, and she told me that the old man across from us had just lost his wife, so we needed to pray for and encourage him. Then she told me that the woman we saw walking by was struggling with bills she couldn't pay and we needed to minister to her." Was God using a small child to minister the gifts of the Spirit in the marketplace?

To channel the anointing through the gifts of the Spirit stretches our faith. We need to use more faith to prophesy or give a word of knowledge than we do to shake or fall down.

Many years ago I was ministering in a church when prophesy and gifts of the Spirit were just becoming acceptable to some people. I felt the Lord tell me that a man in the congregation had just lost his job and was very worried. I was about to tell him publicly when a voice said to me, "If you are wrong this church will close itself to your ministry." I hesitated, but then still felt to continue. Again the voice warned me, so in the end I compromised somewhat, and told the man that the Lord was going to take care of his job situation. After the meeting, he came to me and said that he had lost his job the day before. Satan had tried to stop me from operating in the word of knowledge by putting fear on me, and had partially succeeded.

Spiritual gifts are to be exercised. Like the natural realm, we become more proficient when we continually use or exercise our talents. Some people start well and if they mess up, they withdraw and discontinue to move in the gifts. Even churches can do that if they have some flaky people prophesying or experience some embarrassing situations. It's always more comfortable to rationalize and go back to the safe programs. We must be willing to take risks and make mistakes. If I can't take the glory when I succeed, then I shouldn't take the blame when I fail. It is better to try and fail than not to try at all. That is the lesson of life and it is especially true in the Christian experience. In the parable of the talents, Jesus taught how to invest them to make more (that's a risk). But one person buried them for safety and was severely rebuked. **(See Matt. 25:14-30.)**

CHAPTER SEVEN

Generational Anointing

In this current renewal, many people are excited and amazed that the Holy Spirit has finally fallen on the children. I don't know why we should be surprised. This has happened countless times in history during revivals. John Wesley, the great Methodist preacher had and witnessed wonderful moves of God on children in England in the 1700's. During the 25 years of our ministry, we have always seen the Holy Spirit move on children of all ages. We wrote a book called *Children Aflame* documenting some of the accounts with children in John Wesley's meetings, and some accounts in our own meetings.

One of the most important things for us who have experienced the anointing is to pass it on to our children. If churches are to survive they must also preach, teach, and impart an anointing to the younger generation. They cannot carry on with babysitting or entertaining the kids. Putting them out in a back room or giving them fun and games while the parents have "real church" is to lose them.

God expects us to pass on the baton to our children. To pass on a baton, the person who receives it **must** be running at the same speed as you. If the Holy Spirit anointing is passed on from generation to generation, then the church will stay alive, grow, and fulfill her divine destiny. I have been in many Spirit-filled churches and often found that the majority of children and many teenagers have never had an experience of being baptized in the Holy Spirit with the evidence of speaking in tongues. In fact they have never had it taught to them. Somehow it has **not** been considered a priority for the youngsters. They seem to get a good dose of activities, entertainment, and some religion, but little experience of the Holy Spirit. Why is this?

I will list a number of false assumptions.

They are not ready because:

A. They are too young. Children are never too young to receive the Holy Spirit. *"... He will also be filled with the Holy Spirit, even from his mother's womb"* (**Luke 1:15**). *"... And you shall receive the gift of the Holy Spirit. For the promise is to you and to your children ..."* (**Acts 2:38-39**).

B. They are too immature. Their spirits are often open to receive, even if their minds are not yet mature. *"And it shall come to pass in the last days, says God, That I will pour out of My Spirit on all flesh; Your sons and your daughters shall prophesy ..."* (**Acts 2:17**).

C. We are waiting for the parents to get it first. There have been many cases where small children have been instrumental in leading their parents to the Lord. *"But Jesus called them to Him and said, 'Let the little children come to Me, and do not forbid them; for of such is the kingdom of God'"* **(Luke 18:16).** We had a series of meetings at the Tabernacle Church in Melbourne, Florida. They had been experiencing renewal for many months, but were concerned that the children should also receive. At an evening meeting for the children, the Holy Spirit was poured out in a wonderful way. The following day, a mother came and told me that her seven year old kept her up till 1:00 a.m., praying with her in new tongues, which she had received at the meeting the night before. "She was so excited that she had received her prayer language," her mother said. *"Here I am and the children whom the Lord has given me! We are for signs and wonders in Israel . . ."* **(Isa. 8:18).**

D. We don't have qualified staff to teach them. *"So when they had eaten breakfast, Jesus said to Simon Peter, 'Simon, son of Jonah, do you love Me more than these?' He said, 'Yes, Lord; You know that I love You.' He said to him, 'Feed My lambs'"* **(John 21:15).** Note that Jesus said feed My **lambs** first, then the sheep. **(See verse 16.)** We must conclude that the lambs are the children. Numerous churches have disobeyed the Lord's command by feeding the sheep first and throwing a few crumbs to the lambs. This means that we can't just have anybody to minister to our children, but people that are qualified, dedicated, and anointed. *"Therefore, brethren, seek out from among you seven men of good reputation, **full of the Holy***

Spirit and wisdom, *whom we may appoint over this busi-*
ness" (**Acts 6:3**).

E. It will happen to them when they desire it. Like anybody else, children need to be encouraged to seek the reality of
God. We should exhort them to desire the things of God. *"Train*
up a child in the way he should go, and when he is old he will
not depart from it" (**Prov. 22:6**). Training a child is not "raising"
them. People talk about raising kids in the same way as raising
chickens or rabbits. Children are to be **trained,** which means
discipled. One part of the meaning in Proverbs for training is this:
As a mother or nurse stimulates the palate of the infant so that it
will take nourishment, so we parents are to stimulate the appetites
of our children so that they may feed from God for themselves.
*"Pursue love, and **desire** spiritual gifts . . ."* (**1 Cor. 14:1**).

F. It is dangerous to manipulate children into religious
experiences. This is not a valid argument. Just because there
are certain dangers doesn't mean we do nothing. Preachers make
altar calls all the time. Salvation is a religious experience if it's
genuine. Many children have real salvation experiences. Encouraging them to experience and learn about the Holy Spirit is **not**
manipulation, it is wisdom. It has been our experience that the
same principles that we apply to adults to receive the presence of
the Holy Spirit also apply to children and youth. God's desire is
not for us to have religious children, but anointed ones. Children
can be nice and sweet, but if they are spiritually dead, then they
are in danger of facing hell. *"Then they also brought infants to*
Him that He might touch [lay His hands, anoint, bless]
them . . ." (**Luke 18:15**).

Recently Kathie and I were in Malaysia speaking at a National Children's Pastor's Conference. One of the other key speakers was Clarine Chun, a pastor's wife of Trinity Baptist Church in Alor Setar, Kedah, West Malaysia. Clarine has written several challenging books.

In *Please Do Not Despise Me* she says the following: "Currently newborn babies in our church are encouraged to stay in the adult service. The six year olds and above take notes while the pastor is preaching. They respond to altar calls together with the adults. They pray, worship, tithe, weep, laugh, speak in tongues, and get slain in the Spirit together with their parents. I am very strict with the children and train them to understand that they too are part of the body of Christ. The adult service is not complete without them. Once our church children are past kindergarten age they are not allowed in the nursery. Many of them opt to stay in the adult service anyway. These children do not run around, play, or do coloring in the service. We hardly have problems with children crying, playing, and running all over the place in our church. We believe in them. Children will be what you believe them to be. If our children can sit in school for six hours every day and are expected by both teachers and parents to give their full concentration, why can't we expect that they will also sit for two hours and join the adult service. By the time the children join the youth group, they are ready for leadership."

Clarine currently has over 900 children coming to her Superkids Church; a great number are from non-Christian families. She goes on to say, "I do not run Superkids Church at the same time as the adult worship service. The adult service is from

9-12 a.m. Superkids church is from 4-6 p.m. This gives me the advantage of having quality musicians for Superkids Church. Since we are training an army, they are willing to make sacrifices to come back again in the afternoon for the children. My core teachers do not quit Superkids Church. Year after year, my team of teachers gets bigger and bigger." The children of the families that belong to her church cannot go to Superkids Church unless they attend the adult service. In one of her books, she says the children have learned to enjoy the adult service as much as Superkids Church. Clarine goes on to say, "Like many churches, we have healing crusades in our church. One of my greatest joys is to see the children and the youth laying hands on the elderly and praying for them. The anticipation of the elderly as they wait for the children and youth to pray for them often moves me to tears."

In her book *Not Without the Children* she says that to pass on the **generational anointing,** the children and youth **must** be involved in the main body of the church. Too many churches are losing their children because they are separated from the main body and given fun and games. The generational anointing is not being passed on to them.

I wholeheartedly concur with Clarine. Recently I was preaching and a nine-year-old boy was feverishly taking notes from my sermon. When I do a seminar for teachers, parents, youth pastors and children's nursery workers, many children attend. Critics have said that it is not possible for 6-14 year olds to sit through a five-hour seminar. But they do, and for the most part they enjoy it, because it's about them.

If we have un-anointed teachers ministering to our children, they will not make it. There are hundreds of children that are raised in the church, but by the time they become teenagers they have turned their backs on God and left the church. The anointing **must** be passed on to them. Anointed teaching and preaching with signs and wonders will greatly alleviate teenage dropout.

The account in the Bible of when Jesus was a boy is very interesting. His family had just returned from a religious festival and unknowingly left their son behind. Turning back from their day's journey, they went looking for Him, and after three days of searching, they finally found Him in the temple. When His anxious mother addressed Him about the trauma that He had brought them through and how worried they had been, He asked them why they sought Him, as He had to be about His Father's business. Yet they did not understand what He was saying. **(See Luke 2:41-50.)**

If anybody should have understood her Son's special call on His life, it should have been Mary. "Just think, Mother! You had a visitation from the angel Gabriel who had told you that you were to become the mother of the Son of God." **(See Luke 1:26-38.)**

"Then you rushed over to your cousin Elizabeth and she already understood what happened to you. She even said that the baby in her womb leapt for joy when you were giving your praise report." (Elizabeth was six months pregnant with John the Baptist. The Holy Spirit can even reach babies in the womb). "Then the Holy Spirit fell on you and Elizabeth, and you both had a prophetic Holy Ghost meeting." **(See Luke 39-56.)**

"Mary! Do you remember that when you gave birth to Jesus in the manger, a group of shepherds came into the stable with an amazing story of how they had experienced a divine visitation of angels? They claimed that the angels directed them to the stable announcing who your newborn Son was." **(See Luke 8-19.)**

"After the days of your purification, Mary, you took Jesus to the temple to dedicate Him to the Lord. Suddenly a man called Simeon came in and took Jesus in his arms and prophesied over you and Him. Then do you remember? An old woman called Anna, a prophetess, came up and thanked God for your Son and also prophesied over Him." **(See Luke 2:22-38.)**

"And lastly, Mary, the house in Bethlehem where you were was visited by three wise men laden with gifts for your Son. They claimed that a star in the east had guided them. They were told that your Son was the King of the Jews. After they had left an angel warned you and your husband to leave town and hide, because Herod the king was out to kill your child." **(See Matt. 2:1-15.)**

Mary, with all those experiences and divine encounters, still had a problem understanding her Son when He said, "Mom, I'm really into God," when most boys of 12 were into whatever boys did in those days. If Mary had a problem understanding her Son's call, with all those advantages of spiritual encounters, I know that parents today are going to have to do some real adjusting. How are we as parents going to cope? When our child is different from other children, because he or she is into God rather than video games, football, basketball, Barbie dolls, movies, or rock music, are we going to be concerned that they are not normal?

Many churchgoing parents want their children to be just nice, normal and ordinary, but part of the work of the Holy Spirit is to make ordinary children **extraordinary.** Instead of wanting to be part of the group and conforming to their peers, they will have a greater desire to be conformed to the image of Christ.

Parents! be prepared, that in these last days, the work of the Holy Spirit will touch our children in such a way that many of them will go far beyond us in their spiritual experience. Don't allow your religious traditions and conservative views to hold them back from God's best. The Lord has a destiny on their lives and many will be going forth to disciple the nations.

Strange Acts

Because it is sometimes difficult to get children's attention, God has been visiting them in remarkable ways in order for them to focus in on the eternal things. Even more than falling out in the Spirit or doing carpet time, many are having divine visitations. Children and youth in our meetings have seen angels, been taken up in the Spirit, having visions of heaven and hell. A number have seen the Lord, and had words delivered to them. The result of these visitations has resulted in them becoming very serious about their walk with the Lord and very concerned about the lost. Numbers of them have had a tremendous burden of intercession come upon them. Many children have been involved in praying through the 10-40 window with wonderful results. Esther Illinsky along with C. Peter Wagner has a vision to raise up over two million children to pray through the 10-40 window.

(The 10-40 window is an area of the world mainly in Asia, which is between 10 degrees Latitude N.S. and 40 degrees Longitude E.W. This area, and especially countries like Tibet and Nepal, have been closed to the Christian Gospel for centuries. Up until recently, there have been almost no conversions. Dr. George Otis, Jr., of World Evangelism has been sharing some amazing stories of miracles of healing, raising of the dead; wrought through local Christian converts, which are bringing thousands to Christ.)

In 1994, I was conducting a crusade in Suriname, Central America, with about 30 churches. During the miracle meeting I had about 600 children on the platform with me. I was encouraging them to minister to the vast crowd. They had just been praying for the pastors and now people that had physical needs were being brought up. The children, ranging from six-to-fourteen years, were on a higher platform behind me. The children began to pray for a woman who had suffered a stroke, which had crippled her legs and affected her speech. Suddenly she rose up out of her wheelchair and began to walk and talk. When this happened, the people were amazed. It was not because of the miracle, for they had seen healing evangelists preach many times before. Morris Cerullo and others had held crusades for them, but this was different, God was using the children! The mind-set was being broken.

In 1989, I was in Columbus, Ohio. We held our first children's teachers and youth pastor's seminar. A good number of teachers came from a mega-church nearby. They were very excited about the things I had to share. The leader of their children's ministry said, "I agree with everything that you say, but most churches will **not** go for it, including ours." One of the teachers took back about 40 copies of my book, *Kids in Combat,* to distribute among the children's workers. Apparently the pastor got hold of a copy and after reading it, he removed that young lady from working with the children. He said that was not the direction their church was going. He was **the only anointed one**, with perhaps a few of his staff, to do that kind of ministry. After she left the church and joined another ministry, she called me and thanked me for helping her realize that it was better for her not to be a follower of "superstars."

Paul Cain, the well-known prophet, has said that God is going to use a **faceless people** to bring about a great revival before the return of Christ. He said when the dead are being raised and hopeless cases taken from hospitals to meetings and are cured, news media, like C.N.N., will be running around asking, "Who was the evangelist that prayed?" But no one will know. He also prophesied to us in 1989 that we "will lead parades of ministering children, who will empty children's hospitals, and Shriner's Hospitals. Cripples will walk and all manner of diseases will be healed through the ministry of the children before the return of Christ." We are now seeing some of this come to pass. As we often say, "God is healing the sick through the 'laying on of sticky little fingers' by using the children."

More and more churches are becoming open for this kind of ministry to their children. It is hard for us to keep up with the requests that keep pouring in to our ministry office. God is pouring out His Spirit on all flesh in these last days. Jim Erb, pastor of a church in New Wilmington, PA, has done seminars and has tapes to teach other pastors on how to cope when the children in their church become anointed. Jim's former children's pastor, Helen Beason, started the children's SWAT teams (Spiritual Warfare Advanced Training), in his church. Helen is now traveling the U.S. and overseas showing churches how to set up these teams. These children become prayer warriors, prophesy, move in the gifts, and are able to turn the spiritual climate of their churches around. Her book, *Children of Purpose,* shows how to do this. Both Pastor Jim and Helen's vision is how to bring this revival into the mainstream of the church, rather than hide it in a corner. *". . . Since this thing was not done in a corner"* (**Acts 26:26**).

Conclusion

Church leaders **must** know how to pastor when the anointing is flowing, or when they are experiencing renewal. Please understand, the Holy Spirit doesn't need pastoring, only the people. It is a very vulnerable situation to be in. The pastors or church leaders **must not** interfere with the working of the Holy Spirit, but on the other hand they don't want every "flake" and every "fruitcake" to come into the revival and mess it up. Satan is happy to use anyone, good or bad, to bring disrepute to the work. Not only do they have to deal with the problems that may arise during the meetings, but once **some** people get a taste of the new wine, they become quite goofy without proper teaching.

Because of this, there is a real temptation for the pastor or leader to **tone down** the revival meetings. Fear, and especially the fear of man, will hinder and stop many churches from going full throttle with God. Finding a comfortable niche where everything is now on an even keel seems to be a goal to obtain. An old man of God once said to me, "Although the Holy Spirit is called the **Comforter** I have seen that when He has His way, He makes most people very **uncomfortable**."

I was ministering recently in Nassau, Bahamas, at Mount Tabor Union Baptist Church. This is a full gospel black church, under the leadership of Bishop Neil Ellis. The meetings we had were wild, and Bishop Ellis soon flowed with me, ministering under the anointing of the Holy Spirit. I'm sure a number of people from more conservative backgrounds would have had some problems. Yet Bishop Ellis started the church 12 years ago with 13 people and they now have 3,000. His church strives for excellence, and not only were Kathie and I treated royally, but his large staff are so well discipled in excellence, that many churches in America would benefit from using Mt. Tabor as a role model. The testimonies of healing and financial blessing from his church members were tremendous. The Department of Tourism awarded two people with monetary gifts, saying, "These people exceeded in excellence and had gone beyond that which was required of them and have been very instrumental in increasing the tourism business in the Bahamas." Both of the people were female members of his church. He presented their checks of $550.00 at the meeting amid overwhelming applause.

When revival comes, not only will the pastor have to cope with people that will oppose everything pertaining to the Holy Spirit, but the goofy ones will become a law unto themselves by challenging their leaders, or just doing what they believe the Lord is saying to them at the time. For years, many of these people had **never** heard God speak, and now they believe He is talking to them **nonstop**. They finally have no problem hearing His voice, and usually it's direct revelation to them without any reference to anyone else. God is now telling them what clothes to wear, what to eat, what side of the bed to get out of, or what church to go to. In fact they can't operate unless they get a word from the Lord. The amazing thing is that God tells them one thing and then changes His mind, so you don't know how many different ways they are going, or how many different contradictory prophecies they have received. When the pastor asks them for a commitment to something, they say, "I will seek the Lord and see what He says." Because the pastors, supposedly, are unable to hear from God like these people, they cannot rely on them for anything. When they don't show, it's because God changed His mind, and the pastor didn't realize what God was saying.

Many years ago when we were leading a church fellowship in England, we had some goofy people to deal with. One night a student arrived at our house at about 10:00 p.m. He told us how God had sent him over to us. "First of all, God told me to go and visit Frank, but he wasn't home. Then God told me to visit Brian and his wife, but they weren't home either, so finally the Lord told me to come here and see you." He really believed he was moving in a powerful anointing of divine direction.

Pastors should want to encourage people to hear from God for themselves, but at the same time they want them to have the protection and oversight from more mature Christians, and especially from those that have spiritual oversight for them. Strong leadership is necessary to succeed, but not dictatorship. If he trains people to follow him as he follows the Lord with excellence, as Bishop Neil Ellis, then success will eventually come.

One way to look at it is like this. You can take a toddler and tie him or chain him to a solid piece of furniture. This will keep him safe, but restrict him in his movements. In fact to do that would be cruel. Or you can build a nice safe roomy playpen for him to move around in and experiment.

The church should be like a nice safe roomy place with guidelines, certain restrictions, and borders. This keeps the young, Spirit-filled believer out of the danger zone. But he also has plenty of space to practice and develop his gifts. His mistakes can be corrected and adjusted, and he can be encouraged to continue his walk. If he matures as expected, he will be released from the playpen, and eventually he will be making it on his own. But because we all learn from and need each other, we never make it without some support from the rest of the body of Christ. As we build relationships and continue to have teachable spirits, then Satan will not be able to put a stop to the wonderful moves of God in our lives. In this godly environment, we will continue to live in the anointing.

Pastor, remember to **preach with the anointing**. That means it comes out from your belly and not your head. You may or may not shout a lot. Preachers can shout and scream and raise sand, but showmanship is not what we are looking for, only reality. Ambitious people will use their own power to do whatever works, regardless of the consequences, and self-conscious people will not abandon themselves to the Holy Spirit. Both groups need to be delivered. One from self-importance and the other from self-obsession. Once God touches us by His Spirit, then out of our belly will flow rivers of living water. **(See John 7:38.)**

About the Author

Rev. David Walters was born in England. He was converted in 1959 and became a member of Westminster Chapel. After sitting under the ministry of Dr. D. Martyn Lloyd-Jones for ten years, he received the Baptism of the Holy Spirit in 1969 and soon became one of the pioneers in the "House Church" movement.

During the seventies, David traveled extensively throughout England. Not only did he minister in churches, but also in public schools and universities. Many children and students, including teachers, were saved and filled with the Holy Spirit.

David and His wife Kathie, moved to the U.S. in 1977. David is a popular speaker at national and international conferences. He ministers in many churches to pastors, youth and children's pastors, parents, children and teens. He not only holds city wide crusades and camps for children and youth, but he also holds unique family seminars called "Raising a Generation of Anointed Children and Youth" where parents and their children along with teachers, nursery workers, youth and children's pastors attend. These seminars have so affected the attending churches that many have experienced revival and a new vision has been birthed. He is one of the leading ministers in this field in the U.S. today. He has authored ten other books.

David is president of Good News Fellowship Ministries. He resides in Macon, GA. with his wife Kathie. They have two daughters and two grandsons.

For further information or bookings regarding this ministry,
please write or call:

Good News Fellowship Ministries.
220 Sleepy Creek Road Macon GA 31210
Phone (478) 757-8071 Fax (478) 757-0136
E-mail:goodnews@reynoldscable.net
www.goodnews.netministries.org

OTHER TITLES BY DAVID WALTERS

Kids in Combat

Equipping the Younger Saints

Children Aflame

Worship fur Dummies

Radical Living in an Ungodly Society

Children's Illustrated Bible Study Books
Ages 7-14

The Armor of God

Fact or Fantasy

Being a Christian

Fruit of the Spirit

Children's Prayer Manual

For a catalogue
and current pricing:

Good News Fellowship Ministries.
220 Sleepy Creek Road Macon GA 31210
Phone (478) 757-8071 Fax (478) 757-0136
E-mail: goodnews@reynoldscable.net
www.goodnews.netministries.org

OTHER TITLES BY KATHIE WALTERS

Parenting by the Spirit

Living in the Supernatural

The Spirit of False Judgement

The Visitation

Angels Watching over You

Bright & Shining Revival

Celtic Flames

Columba - The Celtic Dove

Seers Manual

For a catalogue
and current pricing:

Good News Fellowship Ministries.
220 Sleepy Creek Road Macon GA 31210
Phone (478) 757-8071 Fax (478) 757-0136
E-mail: goodnews@reynoldscable.net
www.goodnews.netministries.org